THE NEW DYNAMICS OF ACCOUNTABILITY IN FIRE AND RESCUE SERVICES

THE NEW DYNAMICS OF ACCOUNTABILITY IN FIRE AND RESCUE SERVICES

BY

KATARZYNA LAKOMA
Nottingham Trent University, UK

emerald
PUBLISHING

United Kingdom – North America – Japan – India
Malaysia – China

Emerald Publishing Limited
Emerald Publishing, Floor 5, Northspring, 21-23 Wellington Street, Leeds LS1 4DL

First edition 2026

British Library Cataloguing in Publication Data
A catalogue record for this book is available from the British Library

ISBN: 978-1-83742-138-1 (Print)
ISBN: 978-1-83742-137-4 (Online)
ISBN: 978-1-83742-139-8 (Epub)

Printed and bound by CPI Group (UK) Ltd, Croydon, CR0 4YY

CONTENTS

LIST OF ABBREVIATIONS

ACFO	Assistant Chief Fire Officer
CAA	Comprehensive Area Assessment
CFO	Chief Fire Officer
CFOA	Chief Fire Officers Association
CPA	Comprehensive Performance Assessment
DCFO	Deputy Chief Fire Officer
DCLG	Department for Communities and Local Government
FBU	Fire Brigades Union
FRA	Fire and Rescue Authority
HMFSI	Her/His Majesty's Fire Service Inspectorate
HMICFRS	Her/His Majesty's Inspectorate of Constabulary and Fire & Rescue Services
IRMP	Integrated Risk Management Plan
JESIP	Joint Emergency Services Interoperability Programme/ Principles
LAA	Local Area Agreement
LGA	Local Government Association
LSP	Local Strategic Partnership
NFCC	National Fire Chiefs Council
NPM	New Public Management
PCC	Police and Crime Commissioner
PEEL	Police Effectiveness, Efficiency, and Legitimacy
PFCC	Police, Fire and Crime Commissioner
TPA	Traditional Public Administration

ABOUT THE AUTHOR

Katarzyna Lakoma is a Senior Research Fellow in the Centre for Economy, Policy and Place at Nottingham Business School, Nottingham Trent University. Her research focuses on accountability and governance arrangements in local government and emergency services. Katarzyna holds a PhD in Public Administration and has published in a range of public administration, management, political science and accounting journals. She is the Editorial Assistant of the *International Journal of Emergency Services*.

ACKNOWLEDGEMENTS

This book is based on my PhD thesis, and it simply would not exist without the support of many people along the way.

I want to say a huge thank you to my supervisors, Pete Eckersley and Pete Murphy, for nearly seven years of guidance, encouragement and patience. I am also very grateful to my colleagues at Nottingham Trent University, whose support made a real difference throughout this process.

Thank you to everyone who took part in the study. I am incredibly grateful for your willingness to share your time, insights and experiences. This research would not have been possible without you.

Finally, and most importantly, thank you to my husband, Jack, and to my parents, for your constant support, understanding and for always believing in me.

1

BACKGROUND AND INTRODUCTION: CONTEXTUALISING ACCOUNTABILITY IN FIRE AND RESCUE SERVICES REFORM

ABSTRACT

This chapter examines the concepts of accountability and governance in the context of English Fire and Rescue Services (FRSs). In particular, it discusses the governance landscape of FRSs before and after the introduction of the United Kingdom's Policing and Crime Act 2017 reforms. It discusses the available governance models for FRSs and other reforms that the 2017 Act introduced in the fire and rescue sector. Theoretically, it discusses an accountability-focused reform model based on Romzek and Dubnick's (1987) four accountability types: bureaucratic, legal, political and professional, which can help to understand why governments across the world have been introducing various governance reforms to improve the accountability of public services. It concludes with the overall aim of this book and the methodology employed to gather the data on reforms and their implications on accountability in English FRSs.

Keywords: Accountability; governance; reforms; fire and rescue services; emergency services

INTRODUCTION

Governments across the world have been introducing various governance reforms that invariably promise improved accountability of public services.

This is because governance structures shape the institutional context within which accountability operates and ultimately have implications for how public actors engage with and respond to accountability mechanisms (March & Olsen, 1983).

Over the last century, changes in governance arrangements have been evident in many public services that have experienced reforms based upon the Traditional Public Administration (TPA) approach, New Public Management (NPM) practises, and more recently post-NPM initiatives (Osborne, 2006). Proponents of the two most recent rounds of reform have characterised them as the solution to the problems of previous governance arrangements and outlined various 'promises' that they would bring in terms of improved accountability (Dubnick & Yang, 2011), even though this has not necessarily been achieved. This was the case with NPM reforms when the focus was on the performance notion of accountability. On the other hand, post-NPM reforms have focused on more collaborative and learning notions of accountability.

In practice, public management reforms have created multiple and overlapping rather than simple and individual forms of accountability within the public sector. As a result, public services have been obliged to serve multiple democratic, legal, professional, managerial and civic principals with multiple goals (Piatak et al., 2018; Waardenburg et al., 2020). Two prominent studies on accountability: the 1986 Challenger tragedy (Romzek & Dubnick, 1987) and the Internet Corporation for Assigned Names and Numbers (Koppell, 2005) support this view and demonstrate that satisfying multiple accountability demands can prove to be highly challenging.

Scholars have attempted to classify these multiple accountability relationships. Romzek and Dubnick (1987) proposed the original typology of accountability, based on two dimensions, 'source of agency control' and 'degree of autonomy over agency actions', which has been widely adopted in accountability studies. They identified four types of accountability: bureaucratic, legal, professional and political. Each of the four types focuses on the different nature of an accountability obligation: bureaucratic accountability relies on the performance of delegated duties; political accountability focuses on responsiveness to constituents; legal accountability is based upon legal requirements and sanctions; and professional accountability builds on professional expertise.

The literature shows that the nature and form of accountability in the public sector has been changing and has been portrayed as extremely complex (Lee, 2022). The desire to create more accountable public services through existing or new governance structures has been apparent across many public services in England (Murphy et al., 2019) as well as worldwide (Romzek, 2000).

However, it remains unclear why and how governments, who ultimately direct and control public services, might seek to improve the accountability of public services through governance reforms in the first place, and how these reforms change existing accountability dynamics within a public service.

ACCOUNTABILITY DYNAMICS

Governments often introduce reforms in response to policy failures, crises or scandals, which can expose gaps in accountability. Such reforms may shift emphasis between different types of accountability, as identified by Romzek and Dubnick (1987), and are sometimes linked to strategies of 'blame avoidance', where responsibility for failures is shifted to other actors (Flinders, 2002). Accountability reforms often coincide with policy changes, forming part of broader political responses aimed at addressing administrative problems and managing public perceptions.

When ministers seek to tighter control over policy throughout hierarchical chains, they may prioritise *bureaucratic accountability* and centralise operations to ensure that public services align with government priorities. This approach is particularly evident during crises, such as fiscal stress or the COVID-19 pandemic (Wang et al., 2021), when centralised oversight becomes particularly important.

Alternatively, governments may focus on *legal accountability*, by strengthening external oversight through bodies with the authority to enforce compliance and impose sanctions (Romzek, 2000). This focus was prominent in NPM reforms, which sought to supplement traditional political accountability with legal mechanisms. For example, England's Audit Commission monitored local authorities and allowed government intervention in underperforming areas (Kelly, 2003).

Professional accountability can also be central to governance reforms because it stresses the expertise and autonomy of professionals such as scientists, doctors or economists. Ministers may leverage this to 'depoliticise' contentious decisions and shift responsibility onto experts, as seen in the United Kingdom during the COVID-19 pandemic, when policy choices were framed as following scientific advice (Flinders, 2020).

Finally, governments may wish to focus on *political accountability*, which often involves direct citizen participation and aligns with post-NPM approaches that emphasise co-production and bottom-up participation in public services (Dudau et al., 2019).

The next section will examine accountability and governance reforms in Fire and Rescue Services (FRSs), which is followed by the research context of this book – the implications of the Policing and Crime Act 2017 on accountability in English FRSs. It then explains the overall aim of this book with the methodological approach adopted.

ACCOUNTABILITY AND GOVERNANCE REFORMS IN FIRE AND RESCUE SERVICES

So far, relatively few studies have examined the impact of governance reforms on different types of accountabilities in public sector settings (Byrkjeflot et al., 2014; Grubnic & Cooper, 2019; Hansen et al., 2024). Byrkjeflot et al. (2014) examined accountability in welfare, hospitals and migration; Grubnic and Cooper (2019) investigated accountability in local health and social care, whereas Hansen et al. (2024) reviewed accountability in the higher education sector. They all found changes in accountability demands following governance reforms, which resulted in greater complexity and multiplicity of accountability types. However, little is known about governance reforms in the context of emergency services.

Emergency services management has not received much academic attention (Wankhade & Murphy, 2023). To date, much of the academic literature on emergency services has focused on the police (Murphy et al., 2017) and, to a lesser extent, on ambulance services (Wankhade et al., 2018). Only a relatively small body of academic management literature has been directly concerned with fire and rescue services (e.g., Murphy et al., 2020; Murphy & Greenhalgh, 2018). However, there is considerable professional and official literature that is available and must be considered. Similarly, although fire engineering and industrial relations in fire and rescue services are major areas of academic interest, to date very little attention has been paid to the leadership and management of fire and rescue services.

Building on this gap in emergency services research, the concepts of accountability and governance in fire and rescue services have emerged as a niche area of academic research. While technical and operational aspects dominate the emergency services discourse, only a few studies have specifically examined the recent changes in these areas (Ashworth, 2019; Eckersley & Lakoma, 2022; Farrell, 2018; Lakoma, 2024; Murphy et al., 2020; Taylor et al., 2021).

Accountability

Accountability has not been clearly defined in the public administration and public management research. According to Bovens (2010), accountability is a formal institutional relationship whereby an actor must offer explanations for their actions to a forum, which holds the power to evaluate and issue judgements on the actor's performance. Chapter 2 reviews the literature on accountability in greater detail.

While accountability has been widely explored across various public service domains, the fire and rescue sector has received significantly less scholarly attention. Existing studies on fire and rescue services' accountability emphasise the performance notion of accountability (Carvalho et al., 2006; Kloot, 2009; Taylor et al., 2021). Carvalho et al. (2006) and Kloot (2009) argue that without appropriate performance measures and tools, organisations face difficulties in demonstrating accountability to the public and government. Taylor et al. (2021) supported these views by arguing that centrally imposed and independent performance management measures are stronger in providing accountability than predominantly local tools. Although most of the fire and rescue literature on accountability has focused on accountability for performance, some studies have emphasised the importance of financial accountability in delivering value for money services (Spencer et al., 2019). Building on this, the next section examines governance, a closely related yet distinct concept.

Governance

Governance is inherently political because of interactions between formal and informal stakeholders with different interests. Governance of fire and rescue services, much like accountability, has received only limited academic attention. Nevertheless, governing boards as a mechanism for overseeing organisational strategy are widely prevalent across public, private and third sector organisations (Schillemans & Bovens, 2019). In the public sector, the role of governing bodies is to support and advise on the leadership and strategic direction of organisations, rather than engage directly in their day-to-day operations.

There is an established body of literature on governing boards across the wider UK public sector, including in health (Addicott, 2008; Exworthy & Robinson, 2001; Grubnic & Cooper, 2019; Peck, 1995), policing (Cooper, 2020; Davies & Johnson, 2016; Lister & Rowe, 2015) and education (Farrell, 2005; Farrell et al., 2017). However, findings have been mixed. In some cases, governing boards have been found to make only marginal contributions to strategic planning and decision-making (Farrell, 2005; Peck, 1995), while in some others they have been found to be largely redundant (Addicott, 2008). In contrast, Police and Crime Commissioners (PCCs), who have been solely responsible for governing local police forces in England and Wales since 2012, have been characterised as powerful actors (Eckersley & Lakoma, 2022), which in turn made police forces reluctant to challenge them (Cooper, 2020; Raine & Keasey, 2012). The PCC model of governance is distinct within the English public sector, as it is led by a directly elected individual (the only other example is the directly elected mayoral model).

The use of directly elected individuals as local political leaders has gained prominence in the United Kingdom, particularly following the introduction of directly elected mayors in local government in England and Wales, under the Local Government Act 2000 (Elcock, 2008). However, most English councils have continued under the traditional leader and cabinet model. Nonetheless, the shift towards single-person governance model was intended to strengthen democratic accountability to citizens (Fenwick et al., 2006).

THE POLICING AND CRIME ACT 2017

FRSs are accountable to local communities for their emergency response, prevention and protection. Recently, the local accountability of FRSs in England has been assessed as lacking rigour in many places by a number of oversight bodies (NAO, 2015; PAC, 2016) and politicians (May, 2016). Prior to 2017, FRSs did not have their own external inspectorate, their performance management arrangements were fragmented, and the evidence base was diminishing (Murphy et al., 2019). In response to these accountability deficiencies, the United Kingdom's Policing and Crime Act 2017 introduced a range of governance reforms across emergency services aimed at strengthening FRSs' accountability.

Pre-Policing and Crime Act 2017

Prior to the 2017 Act, FRSs in England were all part of local government arrangements and traditionally answered to their Fire and Rescue Authority (FRA), which comprised one or more local councils within their administrative area. A 'stakeholder' model of a local FRA governance, made up of local councillors accountable to local communities, predominated as the governing body for

the majority of FRSs, before the introduction of the Policing and Crime Act 2017. Members of FRAs were drawn from local councillors elected to the local authorities, typically based on their size and, in the majority cases, political representation (Murphy & Greenhalgh, 2018).

FRAs acted as commissioners of FRSs, although the FRS itself remained as the main provider of the service. FRAs had responsibility for the strategic direction, leadership and oversight of the service, while senior management handled day-to-day operations of the service.

Governance arrangements for English FRSs have historically reflected broader local government structures, resulting in a variety of models. With the exception of London, services were organised as county FRAs, combined FRAs or metropolitan FRAs.

- In county authorities, the council was the FRA, in that FRSs were integrated into the council and the FRA, with one member in charge of the fire services portfolio and a sub-committee to support the portfolio holder who was normally the chair.
- In combined authorities, a stand-alone FRA was established to cover multiple local authority areas, with members of the combined authority appointed by the leaders of the constituent councils.
- In metropolitan authorities, arrangements were similar to those of combined authorities, with members of the FRA appointed by the leaders of the constituent metropolitan councils.
- In London, a body called London Fire and Emergency Planning Authority (with 17 members appointed annually by the Mayor of London) governed the London Fire Brigade until the introduction of the Policing and Crime Act 2017.

Responsibility for fire and rescue policy has shifted between government departments over the past three decades. Initially with the Home Office since 1946, it moved briefly to the Department of Transport, Local Government, and the Regions (DTLR) in 2001, the Office of the Deputy Prime Minister (ODPM) in 2002, the Department for Communities and Local Government (DCLG) in 2006 and before returning to the Home Office in 2016 (Murphy & Greenhalgh, 2018).

In response to the findings from the critical reports into FRSs' accountability (NAO, 2015; PAC, 2016), Theresa May announced a new fire reform programme. This programme included the introduction of the Policing and Crime Act 2017, which, despite its name, amended important parts of the Fire and Rescue Services Act 2004, as it aimed to strengthen governance and accountability across FRSs.

Post-Policing and Crime Act 2017

The Policing and Crime Act 2017 introduced a number of major changes to how FRSs in England are governed and held accountable for their services. The legislation encouraged and enabled, but did not mandate, PCCs in England, who are single, locally and directly elected politicians overseeing local police forces, to take on responsibilities for the governance of their local FRAs and become Police, Fire and Crime Commissioners (PFCCs). Their responsibility was enhanced on the basis of the assumed benefits from PCCs overseeing police forces (May, 2016), which had been established throughout England and Wales in 2012 to replace indirectly elected police authorities because of dissatisfaction with the performance of police authorities and their lack of engagement with the public (Raine & Keasey, 2012). The PCC governance model reflects the equivalent US sheriff governance model (Baldi & LaFrance, 2013; Sampson, 2012).

More specifically, the Policing and Crime Act 2017 introduced four potential alternative governance options, in which a PCC can take on responsibilities for the governance of their local FRA and potentially become a PFCC. They apply to county FRAs, combined FRAs and metropolitan FRAs in England. There are separate arrangements for London (Chapter 3 of the Policing and Crime Act 2017 established the London Fire Commissioner), Manchester and West Yorkshire (combined authority mayors). In ascending order of the scale of change that the various governance options involve, they were:

- *The minimum status quo option*, which results in no structural change, but nonetheless requires Police and FRSs to collaborate more closely.
- *The representation model*, in which the PCC is represented on the FRA and has voting rights, becoming one member among many. This is formally initiated by the PCC and is subject to FRA members' agreement.
- *The governance model*, in which the PCC takes over governance of their local FRA and becomes a PFCC, although the Police and FRSs remain as two separate organisations with separate budgets. It is the governance, not the employment responsibility for Police and FRSs that is merged.

- *The single employer model*, in which a PCC takes over the role of the FRA and becomes a PFCC, and a single chief officer and employer for both police and fire personnel, although the operational arms are still separate.

PCCs can only introduce the governance or the single employer models where a 'local case has been made' (i.e., a business case has been submitted and approved by the Home Secretary). This business case has to demonstrate that the proposed governance change will bring benefits in terms of economy, efficiency and safety of the public. The business case must also include the results of consultations with councils, the local public and other stakeholders. Where local agreement on governance change does not exist, the Home Secretary must obtain an independent assessment of the proposal.

All FRSs and FRAs in England were to a greater or lesser extent affected by these changes. By January 2026, five English fire services (Essex, Northamptonshire, Staffordshire, North Yorkshire and Cumbria) had transferred to the PFCC governance model (at that time no service had opted for the single employer arrangement) resulting in the patchwork of governance models throughout England (Lakoma, 2024). However, North Yorkshire FRS subsequently transitioned to a mayoral model, with the formal transfer of responsibilities taking effect on 7 May 2024. All services that transferred to the governance model have involved either county FRAs or combined FRAs.

In two areas (Cambridgeshire & Peterborough and West Mercia), the initial approvals by the Home Secretary were, however, postponed after opponents sought judicial reviews and the proposals were subsequently withdrawn. All submitted business cases met with a certain level of resistance from local public and stakeholders (Eckersley & Lakoma, 2022). PCCs in several other areas had investigated the possibility of governance transfer but eventually did not proceed with any proposals. Overall, FRSs and their stakeholders were largely opposed to the government's proposals to merge governance of both services. Nonetheless, potential proposals to submit business cases to move to the governance model or the single employer model were clearly encouraged by the government.

In addition to the PFCC governance model, the Policing and Crime Act 2017 introduced other changes affecting the fire and rescue organisational landscape, including an establishment of an external inspectorate for FRSs in England – His Majesty's Inspectorate of Constabulary & Fire and Rescue Services (HMICFRS). HMICFRS introduced external service inspections modelled on police's PEEL methodology (police effectiveness, efficiency and legitimacy).

FRSs' inspections include three main 'pillars' (effectiveness, efficiency and people) that comprise questions about core areas of FRSs' work. The inspectorate assesses each service based on inspection visits, with the analysis and inspectors' professional judgement synthesised into the following grades: outstanding, good, adequate, requires improvement or inadequate. Inspections involve interviews and focus groups with staff, document reviews and collecting relevant data. The inspectorate publishes individual results on their websites and produces national 'State of Fire Reports', which brings together common areas for all inspected services. HMICFRS has also the power to undertake 'thematic inspections' on a specific activity (e.g., FRSs' response to COVID-19 or values and culture in the service). HMICFRS formally reports annually to the Home Office, as the department in charge of FRSs in England, and the Home Office also sets its budget.

The Policing and Crime Act 2017 has also introduced the duty to collaborate with other emergency services, if it is in the interests of their efficiency or effectiveness. This legal duty generated an expectation for emergency services to explore possible collaboration opportunities.

In addition to the changes brought about by the Policing and Crime Act 2017, a number of other governance changes were introduced in the fire sector at the same period. The most important ones included transformation of the Chief Fire Association (CFOA) into the National Fire Chief's Council (NFCC) and the establishment of professional standards body – the Fire Standards Board. Although these changes were not included in the provisions enshrined in the Policing and Crime Act 2017, they had been previously suggested by key stakeholders and the government to improve accountability arrangements in the fire and rescue sector. This means that they ultimately have had an impact on the fire and rescue organisational landscape, along with other changes brought in by the 2017 legislation.

Taken together, the changes were intended to increase accountability across the FRSs and emergency services landscape. This book will examine the perceptions of accountability in English FRSs, where governance arrangements are changing or may change, as it seeks to understand the influence of the Policing and Crime Act 2017 governance reforms on fire services' perceptions on accountability.

AIM OF THE BOOK

This book empirically researches accountability understandings of English FRSs, as it compares FRSs' understandings of accountability before and after the governance changes brought in by the Policing and Crime Act 2017.

Given the complexity and number of interpretations of accountability in the literature, this book is therefore concerned with understanding the concept of accountability from viewpoints within the FRSs. Specifically, it compares accountability understandings in services under the new PFCC governance model and those remaining in the traditional FRA governance model.

This study examines governance changes within FRSs in England to demonstrate how different modes of governance shape both the accountability of public services and how those involved understand and enact accountability. It focuses on four key types of accountability – bureaucratic, political, legal and professional (Romzek & Dubnick, 1987). By analysing periods of governance transition, the book seeks to reveal how shifting governance arrangements influence actors' perceptions and practices of accountability, and how these understandings evolve as governance structures change. Most notably, it shows that governance reforms often result in a complex and overlapping set of accountabilities within public services. Although accountability is difficult to measure, because quantitative measures do not reflect the complexity of governance arrangements within public services, this book demonstrates how governance reforms can shift the emphasis from one type of accountability to another, with changes in one form often having implications for others. Examining these changes contributes to a deeper understanding of the social construction of governance models and of the accountabilities that individuals and organisations both create and are constrained by.

METHODOLOGY

A multiple case study research strategy was adopted to address the research question. At the time of data collection (2020–2021), there were 44 local FRSs in England operating under a range of different governance models (county FRA, combined FRA, metropolitan FRA, PFCC-type FRA, London and Mayor-led FRA) – see Appendix.

This study purposively selected cases according to 'predetermined criteria relevant to a particular research objective' (Guest et al., 2006, p. 61) with maximum variance on the governance models that exist within English FRSs. However, this study sample deliberately excluded London and Mayor-led FRAs due to their distinct and bespoke governance structures that cannot be replicated across other cases. Therefore, this book examines four common governance models in FRSs in England: metropolitan FRA, combined FRA, county/unitary FRA and PFCC-type FRA.

Second, the case selection targeted the presence of the PFCC-type governance model, which significantly differs from the other three governance models (metropolitan FRA, combined FRA, county/unitary FRA). In order to examine understandings of accountability from services governed by PFCCs, the study aimed to compare them with the understandings from the other FRA governance models. FRSs that satisfied the PFCC governance model requirement for selection were then selected accordingly to the type of former FRA governance model. Before the implementation of the Policing and Crime Act 2017, all existing PFCC governance model services were governed by local FRAs. Within the three case studies examining the PFCC governance model, one former county/unitary FRA, and two former combined FRAs were selected as the representative sample. The PFCC governance model sampling did not acknowledge a former metropolitan FRA as only four PFCC governance models (one former county FRA and three former combined FRAs) had been approved and had come into force at the time of data collection (2020–2021). On the other hand, within the three case studies with a FRA governance model, one county/unitary FRA, one combined FRA and one metropolitan FRA were selected to maximally differentiate between the FRA governance model (see Table 1).

Overall, six local FRSs were studied in depth, as this book explored the differences between three cases where a new PFCC model of governance was adopted, and three cases of services that continued to rely on the (post-2017) FRA model of governance.

Methods

This study was qualitative by nature, though it relied on more than one qualitative data collection technique – publicly available documents,

Table 1. Sampling.

FRA Governance Model	PFCC Governance Model
Case Study 1 (combined FRA)	Case Study 4 (former county FRA)
Case Study 2 (metropolitan FRA)	Case Study 5 (former combined FRA)
Case Study 3 (county FRA)	Case Study 6 (former combined FRA)

semi-structured interviews and focus groups – to triangulate the data and obtain a more reliable portrayal of the phenomenon of accountability. Data were collected in a two-phase process. The first phase included collection of secondary data via publicly available sources, whereas the second phase consisted of collecting data and information through primary sources of evidence.

Publicly available documents related to contextual information on governance and accountability arrangements were collected from the services' websites. These included governance frameworks, senior organisational charts, annual reports and statements of assurance. The documents were collected to gain better insights into governance and accountability arrangements within each case, prior to primary data collection.

In this study, 35 semi-structured interviews were held with senior FRSs' officers. The study envisaged a minimum of five senior officer interviews per case study, including uniformed staff and a minimum one non-uniformed member of staff per case study. The participants included Chief Fire Officers (CFOs), Deputy Chief Fire Officers, Assistant Chief Fire Officers, Area Managers and professional non-uniformed managers (see Appendix for more detail on the participants and their roles – their names have been anonymised). The study targeted both uniformed and non-uniformed personnel to gain better understandings of perceptions of accountability from both operational and professional support perspectives. This reflects the typical proportion of uniform and non-uniform staff in FRSs. These individuals were chosen because they were experts in accountability and governance in their services. Questions on the interview schedule explored the implications of the Policing and Crime Act 2017 on governance and accountability in FRSs.

In addition to interviews with senior management, five focus groups and three interviews were conducted with front-line operational staff of FRSs to understand perceptions of accountability at an operational level. The study used two different methods to collect primary sources of data because it was expected that senior managers in interviews would have stronger grasp of accountability issues than front-line staff in focus groups, and therefore hoped that understandings of accountability would be teased out better in a focus group environment for the firefighters. The study envisaged one focus group per case study. Five, instead of six, focus groups were carried out because one CFO objected to a focus group, but subsequently agreed to three interviews with front-line operational staff as an alternative. Focus group size was between three to five members of staff. As with the interviews, questions on the focus group schedule explored the implications of the Policing and Crime Act 2017 on governance and accountability in FRSs.

Data Analysis

Digital recordings of interviews and focus groups were transcribed and saved as separate Word files, then imported into NVivo 12 along with publicly available documents. NVivo stored and assisted in analysing all materials. Transcripts were read and analysed in the order of data collection, grouped by organisation, enabling within-case analysis. Case Studies 1–3 (FRA governance model) and Case Studies 4–6 (PFCC governance model) were then cross-analysed to identify shared understandings of accountability within each model, followed by a cross-analysis between the two governance models to identify differences.

This study used thematic analysis to identify patterns of meaning across the dataset (Braun & Clarke, 2012). The initial codes were derived from the conceptual framework – see Chapter 2. These included forms of accountability (bureaucratic, political, legal, professional, and vertical, horizontal, and diagonal) and were applied to relevant text. A second coding cycle took a more inductive approach, identifying additional data relevant to the study, which mostly became sub-themes. These were refined during the writing of the empirical chapters. Saturation was reached when no new themes emerged (Corbin & Strauss, 2015). The analysis process was iterative, as it involved an interplay between the data and the coding process to refine the sub-themes.

CONCLUSION

This chapter has reviewed governance and accountability arrangements in FRSs in England and has set the context for the empirical analysis that is reported in Chapters 3 to 6. The Policing and Crime Act 2017 has introduced major changes to how FRSs in England are governed and has had a major impact on the accountability arrangements in FRSs. Since English FRSs previously had no directly elected element, the PFCC model of governance, when and where implemented, changes the nature of accountability relationships with local authorities, central government, other emergency services and the public. The establishment of the inspectorate, as well as the legal duty to collaborate, also means that the governance arrangements and accountability relationships in English FRSs have become increasingly complicated.

This book empirically examines accountability understandings of senior management and front-line staff in FRSs before and after the introduction of the governance arrangements brought in by the Policing and Crime Act 2017.

In part, this helps to identify whether the government's vision of enhanced accountability within the fire sector equates with the FRSs' understandings of accountability after the implementation of the Act. Examining these changes enables us to improve our knowledge about the social construction of governance models and the accountabilities that individuals and organisations both create and are constrained by.

The next chapter (Chapter 2) explores a range of academic literature relevant to the study of accountability and governance arrangements in public services. It demonstrates how these two concepts can be pulled together into a framework for the analysis of governance changes on accountability.

REFERENCES

Addicott, R. (2008). Models of governance and the changing role of the board in the "modernised" UK health sector. *Journal of Health Organization and Management*, *22*(2), 147–163.

Ashworth, R. (2019). Commissioners, mayors and blue lights. In P. Wankhade, L. McCann, & P. Murphy (Eds.), *Critical perspectives on the management and organization of emergency services* (pp. 288–302). Routledge.

Baldi, G., & LaFrance, C. (2013). Lessons from the United States sheriff on the electoral selection of police commissioners in England and Wales. *Policing: Journal of Policy Practice*, *7*(2), 148–157.

Bovens, M. (2010). Two concepts of accountability: Accountability as a virtue and as a mechanism. *West European Politics*, *33*(5), 946–967.

Braun, V., & Clarke, V. (2012). Thematic analysis. In H. Cooper, P. M. Camic, D. L. Long, A. T. Panter, D. Rindskopf, & K. J. Sher (Eds.), *APA handbook of research methods in psychology, Vol. 2: Research designs: Quantitative, qualitative, neuropsychological, and biological* (pp. 57–71). American Psychological Association.

Byrkjeflot, H., Christensen, T., & Lægreid, P. (2014). The many faces of accountability: Comparing reforms in welfare, hospitals and migration. *Scandinavian Political Studies*, *37*(2), 171–195.

Carvalho, J., Fernandes, M., Lambert, V., & Lapsley, I. (2006). Measuring fire service performance: A comparative study. *International Journal of Public Sector Management*, *19*(2), 165–179.

Cooper, S. J. (2020). Police and crime commissioners: A corrosive exercise of power which destabilises police accountability? *Criminal Law Review*, *2020*(4), 291–305.

Corbin, J., & Strauss, A. (2015). *Basics of qualitative research: Techniques and procedures for developing grounded theory*. Sage.

Davies, M., & Johnson, J. (2016). Navigating the one-on-one model of accountability: Lessons for police and crime commissioners and chief constables through the lens of principal–agent theory. *Policing: Journal of Policy Practice*, *10*(3), 278–287.

Dubnick, M. J., & Yang, K. (2011). The pursuit of accountability: Promises, problems, and prospects. In D. C. Menzel & H. E. White (Eds.), *The state of public administration: Issues, challenges and opportunities* (pp. 171–186). Routledge.

Dudau, A., Glennon, R., & Verschuere, B. (2019). Following the yellow brick road? (Dis)enchantment with co-design, co-production and value co-creation in public services. *Public Management Review*, *21*(11), 1577–1594.

Eckersley, P., & Lakoma, K. (2022). Straddling multiple streams: Focusing events, policy entrepreneurs and problem brokers in the governance of English fire and rescue services. *Policy Studies*, *43*(5), 1001–1020.

Elcock, H. (2008). Elected mayors: Lesson drawing from four countries. *Public Administration*, *86*(3), 795–811.

Exworthy, M., & Robinson, R. (2001). Two at the top: Relations between chairs and chief executives in the NHS. *Health Services Management Research*, *14*(2), 82–91.

Farrell, C. (2018). Governance matters. In P. Murphy & K. Greenhalgh (Eds.), *Fire and rescue services: Leadership and management perspectives* (pp. 179–189). Springer.

Farrell, C., Morris, J., & Ranson, S. (2017). The theatricality of accountability: The operation of governing bodies in schools. *Public Policy and Administration*, *32*(3), 214–231.

Farrell, C. M. (2005). Governance in the UK public sector: The involvement of the governing board. *Public Administration*, *83*(1), 89–110.

Fenwick, J., Elcock, H., & McMillan, J. (2006). Leadership and management in UK local government: A role for elected mayors? *International Review of Administrative Sciences*, *72*(3), 431–447.

Flinders, M. (2002). *The politics of accountability in the modern state*. Ashgate.

Flinders, M. (2020). Gotcha! Coronavirus, crises and the politics of blame games. *Political Insight*, *11*(2), 22–25.

Grubnic, S., & Cooper, S. (2019). Enhancing democratic accountability in health and social care: The role of reform and performance information in health and wellbeing boards. *Financial Accountability and Management*, *35* (4), 353–372.

Guest, G., Bunce, A., & Johnson, L. (2006). How many interviews are enough? An experiment with data saturation and variability. *Field Methods*, *18*(1), 59–82.

Hansen, M. P., Triantafillou, P., & Christensen, S. H. (2024). Two logics of democracy in collaborative governance: A mapping of clashes and compromises. *Public Management Review*, *26*(3), 635–656.

Home Office. (2022). *Reforming our fire and rescue service. Building professionalism, boosting performance, and strengthening governance*. CP 670. TSO.

Kelly, J. (2003). The Audit Commission: Guiding, steering and regulating local government. *Public Administration*, *81*(3), 459–476.

Kloot, L. (2009). Performance measurement and accountability in an Australian fire service. *International Journal of Public Sector Management*, *22*(2), 128–145.

Koppell, J. G. (2005). Pathologies of accountability: ICANN and the challenge of "multiple accountabilities disorder" *Public Administration Review*, *65*(1), 94–108.

Lakoma, K. (2024). A comparative study of governance changes on the perceptions of accountability in fire and rescue services in England. *Public Administration*, *102*(1), 3–20.

Lee, S. (2022). When tensions become opportunities: Managing accountability demands in collaborative governance. *Journal of Public Administration Research and Theory*, *32*(4), 641–655.

Lister, S., & Rowe, M. (2015). Electing police and crime commissioners in England and Wales: Prospecting for the democratisation of policing. *Policing and Society*, *25*(4), 358–377.

March, J. G., & Olsen, J. P. (1983). Organizing political life: What administrative reorganization tells us about government. *American Political Science Review*, *77*(2), 281–297.

May, T. (2016). *Home Secretary speech on fire reform*. Home Office.

Murphy, P., Eckersley, P., & Ferry, L. (2017). Accountability and transparency: Police forces in England and Wales. *Public Policy and Administration*, *32*(3), 197–213.

Murphy, P., Ferry, L., Glennon, R., & Greenhalgh, K. (2019). *Public service accountability: Rekindling a debate*. Springer.

Murphy, P., & Greenhalgh, K. (Eds.). (2018). *Fire and rescue services: Leadership and management perspectives*. Springer.

Murphy, P., Lakoma, K., Eckersley, P., & Glennon, R. (2020). *Rebuilding the fire and rescue services: Policy, delivery and assurance*. Emerald Publishing.

National Audit Office (NAO). (2015). *Financial sustainability of fire and rescue services (HC 491)*. NAO.

Osborne, S. (2006). The new public governance? *Public Management Review*, *8*(3), 377–388.

Peck, E. (1995). The performance of an NHS trust board: Actor's accounts, minutes and observation. *British Journal of Management*, *6*(2), 135–155.

Piatak, J., Romzek, B., LeRoux, K., & Johnston, J. (2018). Managing goal conflict in public service delivery networks: Does accountability move up and down, or side to side? *Public Performance and Management Review*, *41* (1), 152–176.

Public Accounts Committee (PAC). (2016). *Financial sustainability of fire and rescue services: Twenty-third report of Session 2015–2016*. TSO.

Raine, J. W., & Keasey, P. (2012). From police authorities to police and crime commissioners: Might policing become more publicly accountable? *International Journal of Emergency Services*, *1*(2), 122–134.

Romzek, B. (2000). Dynamics of public accountability in the era of reform. *International Review of Administrative Sciences*, *66*(1), 21–44.

Romzek, B. S., & Dubnick, M. J. (1987). Accountability in the public sector: Lessons from the Challenger tragedy. *Public Administration Review*, *47*(3), 227–238.

Sampson, F. (2012). Hail to the chief? How far does the introduction of elected police commissioners herald a US-style politicization of policing for the UK? *Policing: Journal of Policy Practice*, *6*(1), 4–15.

Schillemans, T., & Bovens, M. (2019). Governance, accountability and the role of public sector boards. *Policy & Politics*, *47*(1), 187–206.

Spencer, T., Hayden, J., Murphy, P., & Glennon, R. (2019). Stating the obvious: Evaluating the state of public assurance in fire and rescue authorities in England. *International Journal of Emergency Services*, *8*(1), 20–33.

Taylor, L., Greenhalgh, K., & Murphy, P. (2021). Accountability for performance in English and Scottish fire and rescue services from 2010 to 2016. *Public Money & Management*, *41*(1), 36–45.

Waardenburg, M., Groenleer, M., de Jong, J., & Keijser, B. (2020). Paradoxes of collaborative governance: Investigating the real-life dynamics of multi-agency collaborations using a quasi-experimental action-research approach. *Public Management Review*, *22*(3), 386–407.

Wang, X., Xiao, H., Yan, B., & Xu, J. (2021). New development: Administrative accountability and early responses during public health crises—Lessons from COVID-19 in China. *Public Money & Management*, *41*(1), 73–76.

Wankhade, P., Heath, G., & Radcliffe, J. (2018). Cultural change and perpetuation in organisations: Evidence from an English emergency ambulance service. *Public Management Review*, *20*(6), 923–948.

Wankhade, P., & Murphy, P. (2023). *Emergency services management: A research overview*. Routledge.

Appendix: Methodology

Table A1. Governance Models in 44 English Fire and Rescue Services as of 2020–2021 (During the Data Collection).

FRS Name	Governance Model	FRS Name	Governance Model
Avon	Combined	Isles of Scilly	County or unitary
Bedfordshire	Combined	Kent	Combined
Berkshire	Combined	Lancashire	Combined
Buckinghamshire	Combined	Leicestershire	Combined
Cambridgeshire	Combined	Lincolnshire	County or unitary
Cheshire	Combined	Merseyside	Metropolitan
Cleveland	Combined	Norfolk	County or unitary
Cornwall	County or unitary	North Yorkshire	PFCC
Cumbria	County or unitary[a]	Northamptonshire	PFCC
Derbyshire	Combined	Northumberland	County or unitary
Devon and Somerset	Combined	Nottinghamshire	Combined
Dorset and Wiltshire	Combined	Oxfordshire	County or unitary
Durham	Combined	Shropshire	Combined
East Sussex	Combined	South Yorkshire	Metropolitan
Essex	PFCC	Staffordshire	PFCC
Gloucestershire	County or unitary	Suffolk	County or unitary
Greater London	Metropolitan[b] (London)	Surrey	County or unitary
Greater Manchester	Metropolitan[c] (Mayor-led FRA)	Tyne and Wear	Metropolitan
Hampshire and Isle of Wight	Combined	Warwickshire	County or unitary

Table A1. *(Continued)*

FRS Name	Governance Model	FRS Name	Governance Model
Hereford and Worcester	Combined	West Midlands	Metropolitan
Hertfordshire	County or unitary	West Sussex	County or unitary
Humberside	Combined	West Yorkshire	Metropolitan

[a]Cumbria Fire and Rescue Service moved to the PFCC governance model in April 2023.
[b]The London Fire Commissioner is a corporation sole and the FRA for London. It is a functional body of the Greater London Authority. The Mayor of London sets its budget, approves the London Safety Plan, and can direct it to act.
[c]The Service forms part of the Greater Manchester Combined Authority (GMCA), which is run jointly by the leaders of the 10 councils, and the Mayor of Greater Manchester. The Mayor is responsible for the overall governance, strategic and financial management of the Fire Service.

Source: Adapted from Home Office (2022).

Table A2. Interviews – Participants.

	Case Study	Role	Uniformed/Non-Uniformed	Interviewee Code	Length (min)
1	CS1	Area Manager 1	Uniformed	01INT.U	33
2	CS1	Deputy Chief Fire Officer	Uniformed	02INT.U	38
3	CS1	Chief Fire Officer	Uniformed	03INT.U	48
4	CS1	Area Manager 2	Uniformed	04INT.U	32
5	CS1	Director 1	Non-uniformed	05INT.NONU	53
6	CS1	Director 2	Non-uniformed	06INT.NONU	26
7	CS2	Director of Strategy	Non-uniformed	07INT.NONU	61
8	CS2	Deputy Chief Fire Officer	Uniformed	08INT.U	45
9	CS2	Assistant Chief Fire Officer 1	Uniformed	09INT.U	45
10	CS2	Finance Director	Non-uniformed	10INT.NONU	47
11	CS2	Assistant Chief Fire Officer 2	Uniformed	11INT.U	58
12	CS2	Chief Fire Officer	Uniformed	12INT.U	43

Table A2. ***(Continued)***

	Case Study	Role	Uniformed/Non-Uniformed	Interviewee Code	Length (min)
13	CS3	Area Manager 1	Uniformed	13INT.U	33
14	CS3	Deputy Chief Fire Officer	Uniformed	14INT.U	48
15	CS3	Assistant Chief Fire Officer 1	Uniformed	15INT.U	39
16	CS3	Chief Fire Officer	Uniformed	16INT.U	47
17	CS3	Area Manager 2	Uniformed	17INT.U	40
18	CS3	Assistant Chief Fire Officer 2	Non-uniformed	18INT.NONU	40
19	CS4	Area Manager 1	Uniformed	19INT.U	59
20	CS4	Assistant Chief Fire Officer 1	Uniformed	20INT.U	57
21	CS4	Assistant Chief Fire Officer 2	Uniformed	21INT.U	43
22	CS4	Chief Fire Officer	Uniformed	22INT.U	70
23	CS4	Partnerships Manager	Non-uniformed	23INT.NONU	31
24	CS4	Area Manager 2	Uniformed	24INT.U	44
25	CS5	Chief Fire Officer	Uniformed	25INT.U	55
26	CS5	Deputy Chief Fire Officer	Uniformed	26INT.U	60
27	CS5	Watch Manager 1	Uniformed	27INT.U	50
28	CS5	Watch Manager 2	Uniformed	28INT.U	51
29	CS5	Director of Prevention and Protection	Uniformed	29INT.U	50
30	CS5	Watch Manager 3	Uniformed	30INT.U	37
31	CS5	Director of Response	Uniformed	31INT.U	53
32	CS5	Director of Finance	Non-uniformed	32INT.NONU	52
33	CS6	Chief Fire Officer	Uniformed	33INT.U	71
34	CS6	Director of HR	Uniformed	34INT.U	69
35	CS6	Managing Director	Non-uniformed	35INT.NONU	61
36	CS6	Deputy Chief Fire Officer	Uniformed	36INT.U	62
37	CS6	Head of Assurance	Uniformed	37INT.U	37
38	CS6	Director of Prevention and Protection	Uniformed	38INT.U	56
				Average length	*49 min*

Source: Author.

Table A3. Focus Groups – Participants.

Case Study Code	No of Participants	Participants' Roles	Length (min)
CS1	4	Firefighter 1, Firefighter 2, Firefighter 3, Watch Manager.	98
CS2	3	Watch Manager, Crew Manager, Firefighter.	50
CS3	4	Watch Manager, Firefighter 1, Firefighter 2, Firefighter 3.	66
CS4	5	Watch Manager, Firefighter 1, Firefighter 2, Crew Commander, Firefighter 3.	73
CS6	4	Watch Manager, Firefighter 1, Crew Manager, Firefighter 2.	58
		Average length	*69 min*

Source: Author.

2

LITERATURE REVIEW: UNDERSTANDING ACCOUNTABILITY IN THE PUBLIC SECTOR

ABSTRACT

This chapter examines the concept of accountability within public sector governance. It traces the historical waves of reforms from Traditional Public Administration (TPA) through New Public Management (NPM) to post-NPM reforms and shows how these shifts have transformed accountability relationships in the public sector. The discussion explores key theories, including principal–agent theory, answerability, managing expectations and felt accountability, while addressing the challenges posed by multiple, overlapping accountability demands. This chapter also examines the different types and directions of accountability discussed in the academic literature, including the Romzek and Dubnick's classification (1987) and subsequent refinements. Furthermore, this chapter analyses governance transitions from hierarchical structures to more collaborative, network-based arrangements, illustrating their implications for vertical, horizontal and diagonal accountability relationships. A conceptual framework combining accountability types and directions is proposed to guide empirical analysis. Ultimately, this chapter demonstrates the growing complexity of accountability in contemporary public governance.

Keywords: Accountability; governance; public administration; types of accountability; directions of accountability

INTRODUCTION

This chapter brings together a body of public administration literature to examine how governance models reshape accountability relationships. It begins by exploring the foundations of accountability, outlining key theoretical approaches and mapping the different types and directions of accountability discussed in the academic literature. The chapter then considers the concept of governance and traces the shift from traditional hierarchical models of public administration to more collaborative arrangements involving a mix of public, private and voluntary actors.

Within this context, the chapter reviews how accountability has developed across successive waves of public management reforms. Drawing on Osborne's (2010) 'tripartite regime model', it examines the evolution from Traditional Public Administration (TPA), through New Public Management (NPM), to the more collaborative reforms associated with the post-NPM era. These shifts have generated increasingly complex accountability environments, in which public officials must navigate multiple and sometimes conflicting expectations.

The introduction concludes by outlining the conceptual framework that underpins the chapter and the entire book, as it guides the empirical analysis. This framework integrates insights from the governance and accountability literature to illustrate how reforms to governance structures shape the nature and direction of accountability in contemporary public services.

ACCOUNTABILITY

From Accounting to Accountability

Despite increased academic attention, there is a lack of clarity around what accountability means. This is exacerbated by the fact that exact equivalent of accountability does not exist in most European languages (Bovens, 2005; Dubnick, 2002; Mulgan, 2000b). For example, French, Spanish, German and Polish do not distinguish between responsibility and accountability. Numerous terms are used to describe accountability, the most common of which is responsibility, and terms closely related to accounting. There is also no agreed definition in the English language academic literature on what constitutes accountability, which has caused terminological confusion in recent years (Behn, 2001; Bovens, 2005; Dubnick, 2005; Mulgan, 2000b).

This lack of clarity might be partially due to alternative international approaches taken towards studying accountability, which depend on different administrative traditions and academic perceptions. Researchers investigating the concept of accountability have attempted to explain it from their own geographical perspectives: American (Behn, 2001; Koppell, 2005; Romzek & Dubnick, 1987), British (Hood, 2010; Murphy et al., 2019), Dutch (Aleksovska & Schillemans, 2022; Bovens, 2007; Schillemans, 2008) and Australian (Mulgan, 2003; Sinclair, 1995). Numerous accountability definitions have built upon one another as many scholars produced their own interpretations of accountability. Accountability is therefore a 'chameleon-like concept' (Sinclair, 1995) which has various meanings to different people and changes its meaning depending on the context and proves to be an ever-expanding phenomenon (Mulgan, 2000b).

This ambiguity is further compounded by debates about the relationship between accountability and transparency. The literature highlights that transparency is an integral part of accountability, yet the two concepts are not interchangeable. Transparency concerns the disclosure of information (Fox, 2007; Mabillard & Zumofen, 2017), whereas accountability is a broader construct that additionally includes the possibility of sanctions when obligations are not met. In this sense, transparency enhances accountability but remains only one dimension of this multifaceted concept.

Theories of Accountability

A range of theoretical perspectives has been developed to explain how accountability operates within public sector organisations. Accountability can be simply interpreted using principal–agent theory. However, there are also two complementary approaches to accountability in the literature, namely accountability as answerability and accountability as managing expectations that are both based on the principal–agent theory (Acar et al., 2008; Willems & Van Dooren, 2012). They largely stem from the Friedrich-Finer debate from the 1940s (Jackson, 2009). Herman Finer, from the London School of Economics, stressed that accountability is based on maintaining external (exogenous) control, whereas Carl Friedrich from Harvard believed that self-control and soft internal (endogenous) values of accountability are sufficient to hold officials to account.

More recently, a new concept of felt accountability has also gained traction in the public administration literature. It stresses that accountability is only meaningful when those who are being held to account recognise the implications of potential sanctions and change their behaviour accordingly (Overman & Schillemans, 2022; Schillemans et al., 2021). A more detailed account of principal–agent theory, the two complementary approaches and felt accountability is given in the following sections.

Principal–Agent Theory and the Influence on Accountability

In TPA literature, the presence of a principal–agent relationship is at the centre of many accountability definitions. Principal–agent theory is based on the idea of a bilateral relationship between the agent and the principal who can hold the agent to account for its behaviour and activity (Bovens, 2010).

The principal–agent relationship provides the foundation for the two approaches. While accountability as answerability entails a single principal–agent relationship, accountability as managing expectations involves one agent confronted with multiple principals with diverse expectations (Acar et al., 2008). Although the latter case denotes a more complex relationship than the former, it demonstrates that both are still characterised as principal–agent relationships, and the two approaches do not have to be mutually exclusive of each other (Willems & Van Dooren, 2011, 2012).

The principal–agent framework is often presented as a model of conflict between the two parties in a contractual situation, with a one-dimensional focus on formal control and sanctions (Acar et al., 2008; Willems & Van Dooren, 2011). Conflict emerges when interests to be served by the agent are not identical to the principal's interest (Philp, 2009). The primary purpose of accountability in this mode is to prevent agency drift through managing information asymmetry and moral hazards between the agent and the principal (Schillemans & Busuioc, 2014).

Although the traditional principal–agent model has been widely adopted, an increasing number of studies have suggested that it is becoming less useful for understanding the nature of the present complex public governance arrangements due to inherent limitations. One general criticism of the principal–agent framework is that it is too inflexible and formalistic due to its emphasis on hierarchical control and formal sanctions (Willems & Van Dooren, 2012). Scholars argue that principal–agent theory cannot capture all complex behaviours in today's public sector arena (Steccolini, 2019). Therefore, it may no longer be suitable in an environment of multiple accountability relationships, if it ever was.

Accountability as Answerability

Accountability as answerability is a traditional hierarchical approach which is also based upon the principal–agent theory. In simple terms, an individual is obliged to take responsibility for their actions and report to the principal (Sinclair, 1995). In other words, it is a formal institutional arrangement in which an actor can be held accountable by a forum (Bovens, 2010). Mulgan (2000b) identifies a number of features of accountability as answerability:

- externality (the account is given to a person outside the person being held accountable);
- it involves social interaction and exchanges (one side seeks explanation and retrieving a situation, while the other side responds and accepts sanctions);
- it implies rights of authority (one side has a moral authority over the body being held accountable).

Nonetheless, scholars have argued that this approach is relatively limited. For example, Behn (2001) suggests that such formal definitions do not take sanctions sufficiently into account. Instead, answerability stresses the aspect of answering, explaining and justifying actions. The primary challenge for accountability as answerability is therefore to explain how it shapes public officials' behaviour through incentives and sanctions.

Accountability as Managing Expectations

Holding someone answerable suggests the existence of prior expectations, against which their actions can be compared (Romzek & Dubnick, 1987). Public administrators have to manage combinations of multiple, different, changing and often conflicting expectations within and outside their organisations (Acar et al., 2008; Willems & Van Dooren, 2011). Koppell (2005) stresses that organisations trying to deal with conflicting expectations within a web of overlapping accountability relationships are more likely to be dysfunctional. Specifically, public organisations are obliged to serve multiple democratic, legal, professional, managerial and civic principals with multiple goals, which can lead to goal conflict (Piatak et al., 2018; Waardenburg et al., 2020). Two prominent studies on accountability: the 1986 Challenger tragedy (Romzek & Dubnick, 1987) and the Internet Corporation for Assigned Names and Numbers (Koppell, 2005) support this view and demonstrate that satisfying multiple accountability demands can prove to be highly challenging.

Some scholars (e.g., Romzek & Dubnick, 1987) suggest that the idea of accountability as managing expectations plays a greater role than the notion of answerability. In their view, accountability as answerability denotes narrow, direct and primarily formalistic responses to demands generated by organisations. Bovens (2010) provides a distinction between the broader concept (accountability as a *virtue*) and the narrower concept (accountability as a *mechanism*). By drawing on the two concepts of accountability, Bovens (2010) suggested that the broader concept is perceived as a set of normative standards for the evaluations of public officials, whereas the latter idea is used to define a more formal institutional arrangement in which an actor can be held accountable by a forum. Thus, accountability as a *virtue* (based on self-control and soft internal values) can be understood as an endogenous type of accountability, and accountability as a *mechanism* (based on maintaining external control) can be perceived as an exogenous type. Similarly, accountability as answerability is limited due to its emphasis on the external authority while disregarding internal personal values, which serve as an additional mechanism of accountability (Dubnick, 2005). The reason why accountability as managing expectations broadens the fundamental notion of answerability lies behind the idea of the constant process of anticipation, identification and definition of expectations which ultimately leads to certain actions, which demonstrates a more realistic picture of organisations in their present complex governance settings.

Felt Accountability

More recently, a new concept of felt accountability, focusing on the individual's expected accountability, has been identified in the literature (Overman & Schillemans, 2022; Schillemans et al., 2021). Originally developed in psychology, felt accountability attempts to combine answerability mechanism with the expected accountability at an individual level. It uses a bottom-up perspective of focusing on individuals rather than top-down approach of accountability of organisations. This study supports these views and combines both answerability and managing expectations approaches to understand perceptions of accountability from individuals' viewpoints.

Typologies of Accountability

As stated earlier, public officials work in a web of multiple and often overlapping accountability relationships. Scholars have attempted to classify these accountability relationships. Romzek and Dubnick (1987) proposed the original typology of accountability based on two dimensions: 'source of agency control' and 'degree of control over agency actions', which has been widely adopted in accountability studies. They identified four types of accountabilities: *bureaucratic, legal, professional and political* (see Fig. 1). Their accountability typology emphasises the nature of an organisation's accountability obligation – '*accountability for what*' (Romzek, 2000). In terms of two dimensions, the source of control in the accountability relationship distinguishes between the accountability being internal or external to the one being held accountable, whereas the degree of control might be high or low when the principal exercises control over the power holder (Romzek & Dubnick, 1987). In 2000, Romzek refined their typology identifying: hierarchical, legal, professional and political accountabilities based on 'source of expectations and/or control' and 'degree of autonomy'.

Bureaucratic forms of accountability are widely used to manage expectations (Romzek & Dubnick, 1987). Some authors refer to bureaucratic accountability as administrative accountability (Bovens, 2007; Willems & Van Dooren, 2011), managerial accountability (Sinclair, 1995) or hierarchical accountability (Page, 2006). Under this model, there is a hierarchical relationship between a superior and a subordinate, in which the subordinate is accountable to the superior for the performance of delegated duties. There is a wide range of bodies acting as superiors who exercise financial and administrative scrutiny. They vary from external administrative or financial bodies to independent supervisory authorities, chartered accountants, inspector generals and internal bodies (Bovens, 2007).

While bureaucratic accountability refers to hierarchical relationships based on supervisions, *legal accountability* systems (sometimes called judicial) involve relationships between two autonomous parties: an agency and a controlling party outside the agency (legislative institutions). The outside actor is in a position to impose legal sanctions and assert obligations. Legal accountability is similar to the bureaucratic type of accountability, in that it involves the frequent application of control to a wide range of activities.

		Source of Agency Control	
		Internal	External
Degree of Control Over Agency Actions	High	**Bureaucratic**	**Legal**
	Low	**Professional**	**Political**

Source: Romzek and Dubnick (1987).

Fig. 1. Accountability Types Identified by Romzek and Dubnick (1987).

However, the source of control in legal accountability relationships is external rather than internal to the organisation.

Professional accountability stresses the power and control in the hands of the skilled and expert members of a professional or an expert group who are accountable for their job to agent leaders. In contrast to bureaucratic accountability, in which the emphasis would be on close supervision, professional accountability relies on standards, values, technical knowledge and expertise in an unsupervised context (Mulgan, 2000a). Therefore, as Romzek and Dubnick noted (1987), the professional accountability relationship is similar to that between a layperson and an expert. It is based on a principal–agent relationship with a knowledge asymmetry between the agents (Sharma, 1997), with the layperson as an individual who has insufficient knowledge about how the expert should carry out their job.

Finally, the key emphasis under *political accountability systems* is on responsiveness. Political accountability refers to a relationship between an elected representative who is directly accountable to his or her constituents. The representative might be an individual politician, for example an MP, a local councillor, a portfolio holder or a scrutiny chair, or representatives might embrace a group of politicians, for example a committee, sub-committee or working party, which might or might not be politically balanced. If the elected representative(s) fails to be accountable to the constituents, they can be substituted in democratic elections (Erkkilä, 2007).

Over the recent years, scholars have, however, attempted to revise the original typology of accountability introduced by Romzek and Dubnick (1987). This is because some believed that the framework missed important types of accountabilities (Bovens, 2010; Lindberg, 2013). For example, Bovens (2010) argued that accountability as *a virtue*, that is perceived as a set of standards, is outside the domain of control identified by Romzek and Dubnick. Similarly, Lindberg (2013) attempted to explain the complexity of accountability relationships through formulating broader and distinct accountability typologies. Whereas Romzek and Dubnick's (1987) typology provides a basis for accountability classification based on two dimensions, Lindberg's typology (2013) helps distinguish 12 accountability relationships using three dimensions (source of control, strength of control and direction of relationship). This more comprehensive classification of accountability subtypes by Lindberg (2013) broadens the traditional typology by including a new spatial dimension that enables us to distinguish between vertical (upward and downward) and horizontal accountabilities.

Some new types of accountability have also been identified by other scholars, including public accountability, personal accountability, social accountability and market accountability. However, it is important to note that some of these types may not apply to the public sector settings or largely overlap with the accountability types identified by Romzek and Dubnick (1987).

A number of authors have recognised that public (or civic) accountability is a type of accountability system that is essential in democratic governance. Sinclair (1995) argues that public accountability provides a more informal system focused towards the wider public, rather than the political system. Essentially, it is understood as a relationship between public agencies who 'should feel obliged to' account for their performance to the public. As noted by Willems and Van Dooren (2012), public accountability can, however, produce discourses that are critical of the state. In such circumstances, it involves the state answering these discourses through a number of mechanisms ranging from public reports to hearings (Sinclair, 1995).

In Sinclair's classification system (1995), personal accountability is also recognised as a form of accountability. This dimension of accountability is driven by adherence to internal ethical and moral values, such as respect for other individuals and human dignity, and for acting in the public interest (Erkkilä, 2007). This brings it close to accountability as a *virtue* (Bovens, 2010), which is based on self-control and soft internal values. Personal accountability is symptomatic of the administrative culture and is based on values and code of ethics, bringing it close to the professional type of accountability. Nonetheless, advocates of rational choice theory could argue that personal accountability does not exist in a public sector setting due to the individual and fixed preferences, instead of the public interest (Kaboolian, 1998). This view is contradicted in the United Kingdom by the existence of the Nolan principles and by similar public sector codes elsewhere.

Willems and Van Dooren (2012) also distinguish market accountability in their typology or classification. In contrast to public accountability, market accountability is applicable to owners or shareholders who call the organisation's managers to account for its performance. The rise of this type of accountability has been influenced by NPM reforms affecting both public and private sectors. In terms of the public sector, market accountability introduced 'business-like' models and an increased focus on public services' performance. In simple terms, there are many publicly owned services and organisations that must operate in commercial or market environments. They are therefore accountable to both the public and the market. Examples include state-owned corporations that operate in international markets, e.g., transport, power or utility companies.

It is important to note that the different types of accountabilities may overlap in practice and are not always co-terminus or clear-cut. Accountabilities are multiple and contingent, and therefore they lead to complex and multiple accountability relationships. The same principal can hold an agent accountable through multiple relationships, have multiple expectations, exert claims through multiple mechanisms and use numerous incentives to shape the behaviour of the agent (Page, 2006; Piatak et al., 2018).

With respect to this study, there are clear overlaps between some accountability types. For example, personal accountability overlaps with professional accountability, since it relies on adherence to standards, ethical and moral values such as mutual respect. Similarly, public (or civic) accountability overlaps with political accountability as it is an external form in which public services are expected to be accountable to elected representatives and the public. In addition, because Fire and Rescue Services do not usually operate in commercial environments, market accountability is less relevant than in other contexts. Given these overlaps and exclusions, it becomes essential to explore how governance reforms reshape accountability dynamics and introduce new complexities.

GOVERNANCE

Governments in most Western countries have been experiencing increasing pressures to improve accountability of public services (Dubnick & Yang, 2011), which has often led them to reform governance arrangements. Studies have often found that such reforms result in multiple demands and associated shifts in the types of accountabilities (Byrkjeflot et al., 2014; Grubnic & Cooper, 2019; Hansen et al., 2019; Lakoma, 2024). Furthermore, accountability-focused reforms are often accompanied by policy changes, in that they both form part of the political response to perceived governance problems within public administrations and the extent to which governments might wish to re- or de-politicise these issues. To understand these changes, it is useful to consider how governance itself has traditionally been conceptualised and how this understanding has evolved over time.

Initially, governance was considered as a combination of classic Weberian-style bureaucracy based on hierarchy, rules and law and representative democracy (Lynn, 2001). However, more recently a shift has occurred in the interpretations of governance due to a number of factors, including financial deficits, economic stagnation, globalisation, citizens' disenchantment with the promises from the state and increased horizontalisation of the state (Frederickson et al., 2015). Traditional forms of hierarchical governance came to be viewed as being too formalistic, exclusive and conservative to respond to these challenges. Governments across the Western world responded by introducing a range of reforms to make administrative practice less hierarchical and more decentralised, with greater involvement of non-state actors in policymaking and implementation. Nevertheless, the responses to the COVID-19 pandemic and bank bailouts have shown that states can always step in when necessary, and act hierarchically, even if they are structured differently (Mizrahi et al., 2021).

Much of the literature does not define 'governance', on the assumption that it is commonly understood (Osborne & Gaebler, 1992). Academics studying governance provide various definitions of this term; however, there is still little consensus about what governance actually means (see Table 2).

More recently, the focus of the various definitions has been gradually shifting from that of control, rules and laws in the 1990s and early 2000s to that of collective or multi-actor interactions in the 21st century. This represents a change in governance debates over the decades, which demonstrates that traditional forms of hierarchical government and accountability based on control, rules and laws have been supplemented by enhanced interactions between stakeholders based on trust, reciprocity and transparency. Political decisions and policy implementation are no longer the sole preserve of elected representatives and public officials – if indeed they ever were. Instead, non-state actors, along with public servants and politicians from other policy sectors, and at different levels of governance, are also involved in decision-making through more informal mechanisms. This has major implications for traditional understandings of public accountability.

Traditional hierarchical governance models rely on providing clear lines of accountability for citizens (Hirst, 2000). New forms of governance, including network governance or collaborative governance, increasingly include non-state actors involved in flexible and decentralised horizontal arrangements, which can contribute to a potential accountability deficit (Mulgan, 2014; Schillemans, 2011). Such horizontal arrangements are largely autonomous and often non-formalised, which means that they control themselves and are responsible for their actions. Actors involved in such governance arrangements are in horizontal accountability relationships, which means that they are broadly equal to one another and are involved at a similar level of decision-making. In these situations, it might be more difficult for voters and elected representatives to hold organisations that are involved in horizontal governance arrangements to account for poor performance or financial

Table 2. Definitions of Governance.

Focus/Characteristics	Definition	Author
Rules and laws	Systems of rule, as the purposive activities of any collectively, that sustain mechanisms designed to ensure its safety, prosperity, coherence, stability and continuance.	Rosenau (2000, p. 171)
	Regimes of laws, rules, judicial decisions, and administrative practices that constrain, prescribe, and enable the provision of publicly supported goods and services.	Lynn et al. (2001, p. 7)
Collective interactions, networks of institutions, stakeholders' involvement	The process of steering society and the economy through collective action and in accordance with common goals.	Torfing et al. (2012, p. 14)
	Self-organising, inter-organisational networks characterised by interdependence, resource exchange, rules of the game and significant autonomy from the state.	Rhodes (1997, p. 15)
	The ways in which stakeholders interact with each other in order to influence the outcomes of public policies.	Bovaird and Löffler (2003, p. 316)
Control	Institutions designed to exercise collective control and influence.	Peters (1995, p. 3)
	The formal institutions of the state and their monopoly of legitimate coercive power.	Stoker (1998, p. 17)
Democracy	Legitimacy measured by international rules and processes.	Franck (1992, p. 50)
Problem-solving	Solving problems and creating opportunities and the structural and processual conditions aimed at doing so.	Kooiman (1999, p. 69)

Source: Adapted from Franck (1992), Peters (1995), Rhodes (1997), Stoker (1998), Kooiman (1999), Rosenau (2000), Lynn et al. (2001), Bovaird and Löffler (2003) and Torfing et al. (2012).

mismanagement because decision-making powers are shared, and public officials are not able exercise direct control over operations (Papadopoulos, 2003, 2007). This shows that increased horizontalisation and decentralisation in the public sector dilutes accountability among multiple actors involved in decision-making and creates uncertainty, complexity and confusion in the public sector (Haveri, 2006; Piatak et al., 2018).

Although new forms of governance with multiple actors can slow decisions due to a high number of veto players (Scharpf, 1988), recent studies show that collaborative governance has many advantages, including improved both effectiveness and democracy (Torfing et al., 2012). This is because horizontal models promote citizen participation, foster public deliberation and give people greater power to hold political elites to account (Sørensen & Torfing, 2018). However, by introducing new actors and redistributing accountabilities, governance reforms also reshape existing accountability structures and add layers of complexity. Understanding these nuances will help to examine how changes in governance influence not only decision-making but also the nature and direction of accountability.

IMPACT OF GOVERNANCE CHANGES ON ACCOUNTABILITY

Over the last decade, the focus of administrative practice has moved towards less hierarchical and more decentralised forms of governance (Elliott et al., 2022) based on collaboration and joint ways of working (Bianchi et al., 2021). These changes raise important questions around the form and nature of new governance arrangements that have been growing in salience and their implications on accountability. This section explains how changing governance arrangements has significant implications for '*accountability to whom*' – it discusses how governance reforms can change the directions of accountability relationships that involve public sector organisations (Bovens, 2007).

Traditional Hierarchical Accountability

Traditional accountability relationships are grounded in a classic Weberian system of public administration. They perceive hierarchies as an appropriate means of accountability (Rhodes, 1996; Strøm, 2000). Traditional accountability relationships thrive best under a number of conditions (Strøm, 2000). First, direct hierarchical (vertical) lines of command must be established between a superior and a subordinate. Second, the relationship has to be complemented by clear demands from the superior (Mulgan, 2003). Finally, the demands have to run in the opposite direction. All these conditions have to be met to call a relationship 'hierarchical'. Management and formal audits are good examples of hierarchical accountability relationships.

However, over the past decades, traditional accountability relationships have been subject to transformations that include more complex relationships including horizontal and diagonal relationships. NPM reforms have led to significant changes blurring traditional boundaries between the public and private sector, resulting in fragmentation, outsourcing and privatisation of public services (Elliott et al., 2022; Ferry et al., 2015; Schillemans, 2011). Other shifts of power from the point of view of the state included decentralisation (more autonomous local government), subsidiarity, the internationalisation of organisations and externalisation of government activities to private and non-governmental institutions (Erkkilä, 2007).

In practice, the post-NPM public sector must deal with dynamic, informal and non-institutionalised forms of accountability (Meijer, 2007). Many scholars (Michels & Meijer, 2008; Schillemans, 2008; Willems & Van Dooren, 2012) claim that hierarchical accountability arrangements no longer appear to adequately fit with the new administrative developments and therefore have had to be supplemented with new forms of accountability, most notably horizontal and diagonal accountabilities.

Horizontal Accountability

Accountability operates in multiple directions. In contrast to hierarchical (vertical) accountability, horizontal accountability is a form of accountability between parties operating or collaborating in the same areas of interest (Michels & Meijer, 2008). Typically, all parties are essentially equal to one another, and more negotiation and collaboration takes place under this direction of accountability. Actors involved in a horizontal accountability relationship get the opportunity to become actively involved at a similar level of decision-making although they do it without a clear hierarchical definition of authority (Willems & Van Dooren, 2012). Horizontal types of accountability emerged during NPM reforms. The labels of 'joined-up-government' and 'whole-of-government' represented these type of reforms (Christensen & Lægreid, 2007; Hood, 2005). However, horizontal accountability has changed its focus as result of post-NPM reforms to greater involvement of citizens in the co-creation of public services (Dudau et al., 2019).

The public partnership model serves as an example of the challenging multi-dimensional accountability relations. In this case, the partnership is accountable upwards to political sovereigns, whereas it is also accountable horizontally to other agencies (public or external service providers) and through elected local government, downwards to the public. An example of these multi-directional accountability partnerships was the Local Area Agreements (LAAs) in England between central government and local areas facilitated through Local Strategic Partnerships (LSPs) (abolished in 2010). In the case of LAAs, they were accountable upwards to central government (via the regional Government Offices and Whitehall) and horizontally to the local authority and local delivery partners, and downwards to the public.

However, scholars raise concerns about whether horizontal accountability can ensure effective control. Michels and Meijer (2008) argue that it can, but only when several conditions are met, including clear responsibilities, well-defined actors, good information flows, open debate and some form of sanctioning. On the other hand, Schillemans (2008, 2011) suggests that horizontal accountability offers limited sanctioning options, while others (e. g., Meijer, 2014) argue that it provides an absolute absence of formal sanctions. This is because actors in horizontal arrangements cannot be removed through traditional mechanisms such as elections or judicial procedures. They are often self-appointed, which implies that exit options are very limited (Mees & Driessen, 2019). Social and professional forms of accountability serve as examples of horizontal accountability relationships, in which the relations are more informal and there might be no sanctions, or the sanctions might be softer or more indirect than in a traditional hierarchical accountability relationship.

Diagonal Accountability

Diagonal accountability relationships are in-between hierarchical and horizontal forms of accountability. They were introduced through NPM reforms to try to improve the efficiency and effectiveness of public services. Non-hierarchical accountability, which includes diagonal accountability, refers to a relationship in which there might be limited or no sanctions; however, the consequences still might be severe (Schillemans, 2008). Diagonal accountability relationships are examples of the relationships that operate 'in the shadow of hierarchy' (Bovens, 2007; Schillemans, 2008), with a two-step relation with a forum, in which a third party is independent from the agent and the principal. The third party is considered as a significant stakeholder to the hierarchical principal–agent relationship. In the first step, the third party, such as inspection bodies and audit institutions, is at one end of the accountability relationship, whereas public services are on the other end. In the second step, inspection bodies and audit institutions act as forums to report to the government and the public on the activities and performance of public services. The government usually does not enforce direct sanctions (other than in extreme circumstances, such as when the law has been broken), but consequences might still be severe for the inspected services (Schillemans, 2008). The government's role is therefore to ensure the public service's legitimacy on behalf of citizens, who are made aware of the outcomes of inspection/auditing processes.

In practice, horizontal and diagonal forms of accountability act as extensions of traditional hierarchical accountability and operate 'in the shadow of hierarchy' (Schillemans, 2008). They do not substitute hierarchical accountability but instead serve as an addition to traditional forms of accountability (Kettl, 2015; Michels & Meijer, 2008; Schillemans, 2008, 2011).

CONCEPTUAL FRAMEWORK

A review of the literature suggests that reforming governance arrangements has significant implications for accountability. Indeed, as we have seen, an underlying rationale for many NPM and post-NPM reforms over recent decades has, inter alia, been a desire to improve public service accountability, even though this has not always been achieved. As Romzek (2000) argues, in times of reform there are usually calls for a reliance on a '*different kind*' of accountability. This was the case with NPM reforms when the focus was on the performance notions of accountability and the public choice critique of government-provided services. On the other hand, post-NPM reforms have focused on more collaborative and learning notions of accountability. This suggests that the key to investigating accountability under different reform programmes is not understanding whether they enhance accountability or not. Instead, it is important to understand what kind of accountability is perceived as appropriate by different actors (Romzek, 2000).

The conceptual framework brings together key concepts from both the governance and accountability literature to organise and interpret empirical findings in Chapters 3 to 6. Fig. 2 illustrates how this framework can help us to understand how the focus on different accountability types may have changed as a result of governance reforms in public services. This study

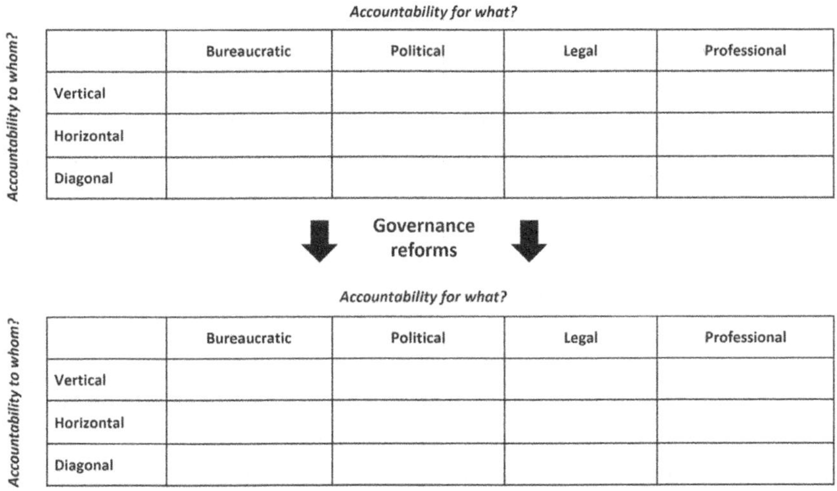

Source: Adapted from Romzek and Dubnick (1987) and Bovens (2007).

Fig. 2. Conceptual Framework.

acknowledges that accountability is often perceived in terms of two dimensions – '*accountability for what*' and '*accountability to whom*' (Pilon & Brouard, 2023) – and uses them both to explain the impact of governance reforms on understandings of accountability. '*Accountability for what*' stresses the nature of an organisation's accountability obligation, whereas '*accountability to whom*' demonstrates the relationship between the organisation and other stakeholders. The framework helps to identify how understandings of accountability may change in relation to both dimensions as a result of governance reforms.

The conceptual framework uses the most prominent accountability typology by Romzek and Dubnick (1987) (bureaucratic accountability, political accountability, legal accountability and professional accountability) as the '*accountability for what*' dimension. Each of the four types of accountabilities focuses on the different nature of an accountability obligation: bureaucratic accountability relies on the performance of delegated duties; political accountability focuses on responsiveness to citizens; legal accountability is based upon legal requirements and sanctions; and professional accountability builds on professional expertise. As discussed earlier, other types of accountabilities are outside the scope of this study.

The framework also employs the second dimension of accountability – '*accountability to whom*' – to examine the impact of governance structures on accountability. It utilises the three accountability directions identified by Bovens (2007) – vertical, horizontal and diagonal. As previously explained, traditional accountability relationships, based on vertical structures in which the forum formally wields power over the actor, have been challenged in both theory and practice (Bovens, 2007), and other forms of accountability have been recognised, including horizontal and diagonal accountabilities. Horizontal accountability relationships rely on mutual accountability between organisations, while diagonal accountability relationships are an intermediary form, where there are no powers to enforce the compliance. '*Accountability to whom*' therefore illustrates to whom the organisation is accountable and the direction of the relationship in which the organisation is involved.

Although the existing literature has primarily focused on explaining accountability types in relation to the traditional vertical directions of accountability, this study extends the previous research on accountability by taking into account all three directions of accountability to understand complex governance arrangements and their potential impact on accountability in public sector settings.

As such, this framework combines the approaches of both Romzek and Dubnick (1987) and Bovens (2007) to examine how changes in governance structures affect understandings of accountability in public services. It illustrates how the accountability types and directions may change as result of governance reforms.

The nature of accountability depends on governance arrangements. The framework enables readers to identify how governance changes affect understandings of accountability. For example, governance reforms might involve the establishment of an external inspectorate, which is a form of diagonal accountability, whereas introducing additional reporting mechanisms to central government might be perceived as changing a vertical accountability relationship. Both examples theoretically demonstrate bureaucratic and legal types of accountabilities, as they involve external institutions holding an agent to account for performance and reporting. However, these are only theoretical examples of how accountability may change. Building on the notion of felt accountability, and the idea that accountability only functions in practice, when those being held to account behave differently in response to the threat of sanctions, it is important to understand how individual actors perceive how the nature of accountability may be changing. This provides new insights into how governance structures that are in flux or operate under uncertain conditions can shape actors' understandings of accountability.

CONCLUSION

This chapter has explored a range of academic literature relevant to the study of accountability and governance arrangements in public services. It has shown that the two concepts can be pulled together into a framework for analysis of governance changes on accountability. The public administration literature shows how public services have moved towards various decentralised forms of governance based on collaboration and joint ways of working (Bianchi et al., 2021; Elliott et al., 2022). As such, public services are increasingly operating in a complex patchwork of governance arrangements and have to manage combinations of multiple accountability types within and outside their organisations in an increasingly changing politicised context.

Drawing on the accountability typology introduced by Romzek and Dubnick (1987) and the accountability directions articulated by Bovens (2007), this chapter has created a framework to study how such governance reforms affect understandings of accountability. Chapters 3, 4, 5 and 6 use the analytical framework to empirically explore accountability in Fire and Rescue Services before and after the introduction of new governance arrangements brought in by the Policing and Crime Act 2017. These chapters discuss four accountability types – bureaucratic, political, legal and professional (‘*accountability for what*’) – in relation to vertical, horizontal and diagonal accountability (‘*accountability to whom*’).

REFERENCES

Acar, M., Guo, C., & Yang, K. (2008). Accountability when hierarchical authority is absent: Views from public–private partnership practitioners. *The American Review of Public Administration*, *38*(1), 3–23.

Aleksovska, M., & Schillemans, T. (2022). Dissecting multiple accountabilities: A problem of multiple forums or of conflicting demands? *Public Administration*, *100*(3), 711–736.

Behn, R. D. (2001). *Rethinking democratic accountability*. Brookings Institution Press.

Bianchi, C., Nasi, G., & Rivenbark, W. C. (2021). Implementing collaborative governance: Models, experiences, and challenges. *Public Management Review*, *23*(11), 1581–1589.

Bovaird, T., & Löffler, E. (2003). Evaluating the quality of public governance: Indicators, models and methodologies. *International Review of Administrative Sciences*, *69*(3), 313–328.

Bovens, M. (2005). The concept of public accountability. In E. Ferlie, L. E. LynnJr., & C. Pollitt (Eds.), *The Oxford handbook of public management* (pp. 182–208). Oxford University Press.

Bovens, M. (2007). Analysing and assessing accountability: A conceptual framework. *European Law Journal*, *13*(4), 447–468.

Bovens, M. (2010). Two concepts of accountability: Accountability as a virtue and as a mechanism. *West European Politics*, *33*(5), 946–967.

Byrkjeflot, H., Christensen, T., & Lægreid, P. (2014). The many faces of accountability: Comparing reforms in welfare, hospitals and migration. *Scandinavian Political Studies*, *37*(2), 171–195.

Christensen, T., & Lægreid, P. (2007). The whole-of-government approach to public sector reform. *Public Administration Review*, *67*(6), 1059–1066.

Dubnick, M. (2005). Accountability and the promise of performance: In search of the mechanisms. *Public Performance and Management Review*, *28* (3), 376–417.

Dubnick, M. J. (2002). *Seeking salvation for accountability*. Paper presented at the Annual Meeting of the American Political Science Association, Boston, MA.

Dubnick, M. J., & Yang, K. (2011). The pursuit of accountability: Promises, problems, and prospects. In D. C. Menzel & H. E. White (Eds.), *The state of public administration: Issues, challenges and opportunities* (pp. 171–186). Routledge.

Dudau, A., Glennon, R., & Verschuere, B. (2019). Following the yellow brick road? (Dis)enchantment with co-design, co-production and value co-creation in public services. *Public Management Review*, *21*(11), 1577–1594.

Elliott, I. C., Bottom, K. A., Carmichael, P., Liddle, J., Martin, S., & Pyper, R. (2022). The fragmentation of public administration: Differentiated and decentered governance in the (dis) United Kingdom. *Public Administration*, *100*(1), 98–115.

Erkkilä, T. (2007). Governance and accountability—A shift in conceptualisation. *Public Administration Quarterly*, *31*(1), 1–38.

Ferry, L., Eckersley, P., & Zakaria, Z. (2015). Accountability and transparency in English local government: Moving from 'matching parts' to 'awkward couple'. *Financial Accountability and Management, 31*(3), 345–361.

Fox, J. (2007). The uncertain relationship between transparency and accountability. *Development in Practice, 17*(4–5), 663–671.

Franck, T. M. (1992). The emerging right to democratic governance. *American Journal of International Law, 86*(1), 46–91.

Frederickson, H. G., Smith, K. B., Larimer, C. W., & Licari, M. J. (2015). *The public administration theory primer.* Westview Press.

Grubnic, S., & Cooper, S. (2019). Enhancing democratic accountability in health and social care: The role of reform and performance information in Health and Wellbeing Boards. *Financial Accountability and Management, 35*(4), 353–372.

Hansen, H. F., Geschwind, L., Kivistö, J., Pekkola, E., Pinheiro, R., & Pulkkinen, K. (2019). Balancing accountability and trust: University reforms in the Nordic countries. *Higher Education, 78*, 557–573.

Haveri, A. (2006). Complexity in local government change: Limits to rational reforming. *Public Management Review, 8*(1), 31–46.

Hirst, P. (2000). Democracy and governance. In J. Pierre (Ed.), *Debating governance: Authority, steering, and democracy* (pp. 13–35). Oxford University Press.

Hood, C. (2005). The idea of joined-up government: A historical perspective. In V. Bogdanor (Ed.), *Joined-up government* (pp. 19–42). Oxford University Press for the British Academy.

Hood, C. (2010). Accountability and transparency: Siamese twins, matching parts, awkward couple? *West European Politics, 33*(5), 989–1009.

Jackson, M. (2009). Responsibility versus accountability in the Friedrich–Finer debate. *Journal of Management History, 15*(1), 66–77.

Kaboolian, L. (1998). The new public management: Challenging the boundaries of the management vs. administration debate. *Public Administration Review, 58*(3), 189–193.

Kettl, D. F. (2015). *The transformation of governance: Public administration for the twenty-first century* (2nd ed.). Johns Hopkins University Press.

Kooiman, J. (1999). Social-political governance: Overview, reflections and design. *Public Management*, *1*(1), 67–92.

Koppell, J. G. (2005). Pathologies of accountability: ICANN and the challenge of "multiple accountabilities disorder" *Public Administration Review*, *65*(1), 94–108.

Lakoma, K. (2024). A comparative study of governance changes on the perceptions of accountability in Fire and Rescue Services in England. *Public Administration*, *102*(1), 3–20.

Lindberg, S. I. (2013). Mapping accountability: Core concept and subtypes. *International Review of Administrative Sciences*, *79*(2), 202–226.

Lynn, L., Heinrich, C., & Hill, C. (2001). *Improving governance: A new logic for empirical research*. Georgetown University Press.

Lynn, L. E., Jr. (2001). The myth of the bureaucratic paradigm: What traditional public administration really stood for. *Public Administration Review*, *61*(2), 144–160.

Mabillard, V., & Zumofen, R. (2017). The complex relationship between transparency and accountability: A synthesis and contribution to existing frameworks. *Public Policy and Administration*, *32*(2), 110–129.

Mees, H., & Driessen, P. (2019). A framework for assessing the accountability of local governance arrangements for adaptation to climate change. *Journal of Environmental Planning and Management*, *62*(4), 671–691.

Meijer, A. (2014). Transparency. In M. Bovens, R. E. Goodin, & T. Schillemans (Eds.), *The Oxford handbook of public accountability* (pp. 507–524). Oxford University Press.

Meijer, A. J. (2007). Publishing public performance results on the internet: Do stakeholders use the internet to hold Dutch public service organizations to account? *Government Information Quarterly*, *24*(1), 165–185.

Michels, A., & Meijer, A. (2008). Safeguarding public accountability in horizontal government. *Public Management Review*, *10*(2), 165–173.

Mizrahi, S., Vigoda-Gadot, E., & Cohen, N. (2021). How well do they manage a crisis? The government's effectiveness during the COVID-19 pandemic. *Public Administration Review*, *81*(6), 1120–1130.

Mulgan, R. (2000a). Comparing accountability in the public and private sectors. *Australian Journal of Public Administration*, *59*(1), 87–97.

Mulgan, R. (2000b). Accountability': An ever-expanding concept? *Public Administration*, *78*(3), 555–573.

Mulgan, R. (2003). *Holding power to account: Accountability in modern democracies*. Palgrave Macmillan.

Mulgan, R. (2014). Accountability deficits. In M. Bovens, R. E. Goodin, & T. Schillemans (Eds.), *The Oxford handbook of public accountability* (pp. 545–554). Oxford University Press.

Murphy, P., Ferry, L., Glennon, R., & Greenhalgh, K. (2019). *Public service accountability: Rekindling a debate*. Springer.

Osborne, D., & Gaebler, T. (1992). *Reinventing government: How the entrepreneurial spirit is transforming the public sector from schoolhouse to statehouse*. Addison-Wesley.

Osborne, S. (Ed.). (2010), *The new public governance? Emerging perspectives on the theory and practice of public governance*. Routledge.

Overman, S., & Schillemans, T. (2022). Toward a public administration theory of felt accountability. *Public Administration Review*, *82*(1), 12–22.

Page, S. (2006). The web of managerial accountability: The impact of reinventing government. *Administration & Society*, *38*(2), 166–197.

Papadopoulos, Y. (2003). Cooperative forms of governance: Problems of democratic accountability in complex environments. *European Journal of Political Research*, *42*(4), 473–501.

Papadopoulos, Y. (2007). Problems of democratic accountability in network and multilevel governance. *European Law Journal*, *13*(4), 469–486.

Peters, B. G. (1995). Bureaucracy in a divided regime: The United States. In J. Pierre (Ed.), *Bureaucracy in the modern state: An introduction to comparative administration* (pp. 18–38). Edward Elgar.

Philp, M. (2009). Delimiting democratic accountability. *Political Studies*, *57* (1), 28–53.

Piatak, J., Romzek, B., LeRoux, K., & Johnston, J. (2018). Managing goal conflict in public service delivery networks: Does accountability move up and down, or side to side? *Public Performance and Management Review*, *41* (1), 152–176.

Pilon, M., & Brouard, F. (2023). Conceptualizing accountability as an integrated system of relationships, governance, and information. *Financial Accountability and Management*, *39*(2), 421–446.

Rhodes, R. A. W. (1996). The new governance: Governing without government. *Political Studies*, *44*(4), 652–667.

Rhodes, R. A. W. (1997). *Understanding governance: Policy networks, governance, reflexivity and accountability*. Open University Press.

Romzek, B. (2000). Dynamics of public accountability in the era of reform. *International Review of Administrative Sciences*, *66*(1), 21–44.

Romzek, B. S., & Dubnick, M. J. (1987). Accountability in the public sector: Lessons from the Challenger tragedy. *Public Administration Review*, *47*(3), 227–238.

Rosenau, J. N. (2000). Change, complexity and governance in globalizing space. In J. Pierre (Ed.), *Debating governance: Authority, steering and democracy* (pp. 167–200). Oxford University Press.

Scharpf, F. W. (1988). The joint-decision trap: Lessons from German federalism and European integration. *Public Administration*, *66*(3), 239–278.

Schillemans, T. (2008). Accountability in the shadow of hierarchy: The horizontal accountability of agencies. *Public Organization Review*, *8*, 175–194.

Schillemans, T. (2011). Does horizontal accountability work? Evaluating potential remedies for the accountability deficit of agencies. *Administration & Society*, *43*(4), 387–416.

Schillemans, T., & Busuioc, M. (2014). Predicting public sector accountability: From agency drift to forum drift. *Journal of Public Administration Research and Theory*, *25*(1), 191–215.

Schillemans, T., Overman, S., Fawcett, P., Flinders, M., Fredriksson, M., Laegreid, P., Maggetti, M., Papadopoulos, Y., Rubecksen, K., Rykkja, L. H., & Salomonsen, H. H. (2021). Understanding felt accountability: The institutional antecedents of the felt accountability of agency CEOs to central government. *Governance*, *34*(3), 893–916.

Sharma, A. (1997). Professional as agent: Knowledge asymmetry in agency exchange. *Academy of Management Review*, *22*(3), 758–798.

Sinclair, A. (1995). The chameleon of accountability: Forms and discourses. *Accounting, Organizations and Society*, *20*(2), 219–237.

Sørensen, E., & Torfing, J. (2018). The democratizing impact of governance networks: From pluralization, via democratic anchorage, to interactive political leadership. *Public Administration*, *96*(2), 302–317.

Steccolini, I. (2019). Accounting and the post-new public management: Re-considering publicness in accounting research. *Accounting, Auditing & Accountability Journal*, *32*(1), 255–279.

Stoker, G. (1998). Governance as theory: Five propositions. *International Social Science Journal*, *50*(155), 17–28.

Strøm, K. (2000). Delegation and accountability in parliamentary democracies. *European Journal of Political Research*, *37*(3), 261–290.

Torfing, J., Peters, B. G., Pierre, J., & Sørensen, E. (2012). *Interactive governance: Advancing the paradigm*. Oxford University Press.

Waardenburg, M., Groenleer, M., de Jong, J., & Keijser, B. (2020). Paradoxes of collaborative governance: Investigating the real-life dynamics of multi-agency collaborations using a quasi-experimental action-research approach. *Public Management Review*, *22*(3), 386–407.

Willems, T., & Van Dooren, W. (2011). Lost in diffusion? How collaborative arrangements lead to an accountability paradox. *International Review of Administrative Sciences*, *77*(3), 505–530.

Willems, T., & Van Dooren, W. (2012). Coming to terms with accountability: Combining multiple forums and functions. *Public Management Review*, *14*(7), 1011–1036.

3

FINDINGS: BUREAUCRATIC ACCOUNTABILITY

ABSTRACT

This chapter examines the dynamics of bureaucratic accountability within English Fire and Rescue Services (FRSs) before and after the governance reforms introduced by the Policing and Crime Act 2017. Using Romzek and Dubnick's (1987) framework, it explores vertical, horizontal and diagonal accountability relationships and their changes under different governance structures. Prior to 2017, accountability was primarily exercised through Fire and Rescue Authorities (FRAs), whose scrutiny was often limited by local councillors' lack of expertise and competing priorities. The Act introduced new arrangements, including Police, Fire and Crime Commissioners (PFCCs), statutory collaboration duties and the establishment of His Majesty's Inspectorate of Constabulary and Fire & Rescue Services (HMICFRS). These reforms strengthened oversight, formalised inter-agency collaboration and re-introduced external performance inspections, while also creating tensions around operational independence and increasing bureaucratic demands. This chapter concludes that the 2017 legislation enhanced bureaucratic accountability mechanisms but also introduced challenges such as governance complexity and increased administrative burden on FRSs.

Keywords: Bureaucratic accountability; fire and rescue services; governance reform; public administration; directions of accountability

INTRODUCTION

As Chapter 1 clarified, this book focuses on the dynamics of accountability in English Fire and Rescue Services (FRSs), where perceptions of accountability change as a result of governance reforms introduced by the Policing and Crime Act 2017. It uses the conceptual framework introduced in Chapter 2 (*'accountability for what'* and *'accountability to whom'*) to examine the empirical findings on the dynamics of accountability in FRSs. This chapter focuses on one of the four types of accountability identified by Romzek and Dubnick (1987), namely bureaucratic accountability.

Bureaucratic forms of accountability are widely used to manage expectations (Romzek & Dubnick, 1987). Some scholars refer to bureaucratic accountability as administrative accountability (Bovens, 2007; Willems & Van Dooren, 2011), hierarchical accountability (Romzek, 2000) or managerial accountability (Sinclair, 1995). Under this model, there is a principal–agent relationship between a superior and a subordinate, in which the subordinate is accountable to the superior for the performance of delegated duties. A wide range of bodies act as superiors who exercise scrutiny. They vary from external administrative to independent supervisory authorities, chartered accountants, inspector generals and internal bodies (Bovens, 2007).

FRSs are a type of hierarchical organisations, which means that they are in bureaucratic, supervisory control relationships with a number of internal and external stakeholders. This chapter describes FRSs' understandings of bureaucratic accountability in relation to the vertical, horizontal and diagonal directions of accountability to address the *'accountability for what'* and *'accountability to whom'* dimensions of the conceptual framework. More specifically, it examines how these understandings have changed in the context of the governance reforms brought in by the Policing and Crime Act 2017 (see Figs. 3 and 4).

ACCOUNTABILITY ARRANGEMENTS PRIOR TO THE POLICING AND CRIME ACT 2017

Vertical Accountability

In a vertical accountability relationship, a superior is calling for an account from those who are accountable (subordinate), including the rights to demand answers and to impose sanctions. Vertical accountability relationships feature direct vertical lines of command between a superior and a subordinate, with

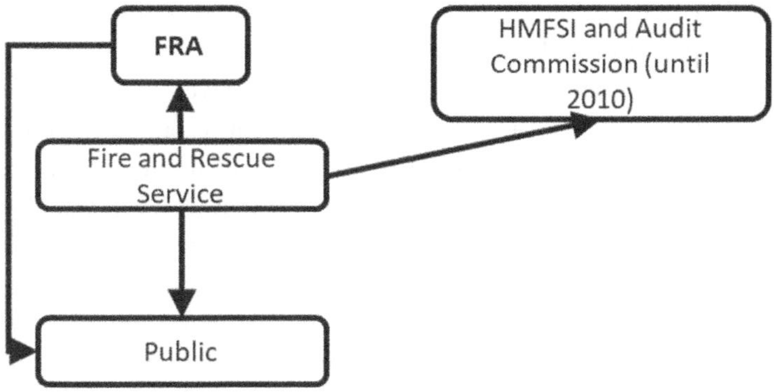

Source: Author's interpretation.

Fig. 3. Fire and Rescue Services' Understandings on Bureaucratic Accountability Relationships in FRA-Governed Fire and Rescue Services Before the Introduction of the Policing and Crime Act 2017.

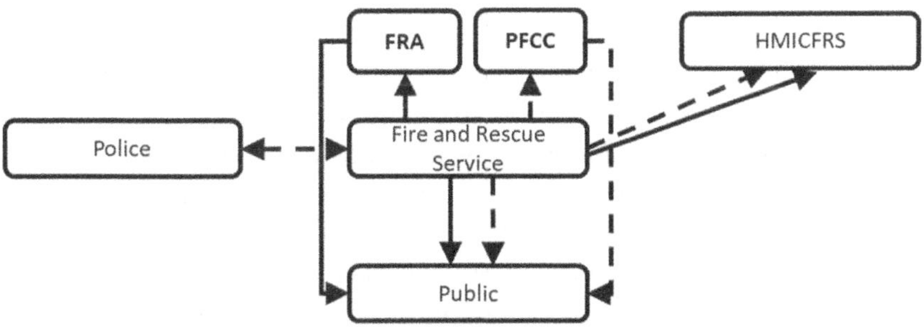

Source: Author's interpretation.

Fig. 4. Fire and Rescue Services' Understandings on Bureaucratic Accountability Relationships in FRA-Governed (Solid Lines) and in PFCC-Governed (Dotted Lines) Fire and Rescue Services After the Introduction of the Policing and Crime Act 2017.

clear demands from the superior (Mulgan, 2003). This subsection covers the sub-themes of overview and scrutiny, and performance management, which emerged from the data analysis on the vertical dimension of bureaucratic accountability.

Overview and Scrutiny

An executive model of decision-making was introduced by the Local Government Act 2000, which distinguished between executive decision-making and overview and scrutiny in local government. In the context of FRSs, Fire and Rescue Authorities (FRAs) have been carrying out the role of overview and scrutiny, which means that they have the power to scrutinise the decision-making of their local FRS and make relevant recommendations. More specifically, FRAs' strategic role is to oversee FRSs' organisational strategy and approve statutory documents, including the Integrated Risk Management Plan (IRMP), the Annual Statement of Assurance and financial plans. This in turn means that FRSs are bureaucratically accountable to their corresponding FRAs. FRAs consist of approximately 15–20 members that are drawn from local councillors elected to the local authorities within the administrative areas. The FRAs operate with a number of committees that sit under the FRAs to make decisions on key FRSs' operational matters, such as strategy, policy and budgets. The FRAs meet four times a year, usually once a quarter.

Notwithstanding the FRA's statutory responsibilities, senior managers had mixed views on the actual ability of FRAs to challenge their local FRSs. In the interviews, they largely indicated that their FRA had insufficiently scrutinised their service. They attributed this primarily to local councillors' other commitments that required substantially more of their time and interest than their local FRSs. This was particularly notable in the services that were an integral part of county council arrangements, where FRSs were perceived as having a lower profile than other public services, such as social care, education, public health and highways. Local councillors often relegated the FRS' matters to a secondary priority, on the assumption that other services were more important or more interesting. This lack of attention was further reflected in the absence of 'specific' independent scrutiny committees for FRSs. Although such committees are supposed to provide independent oversight of the FRSs' performance, the evidence suggests that some FRSs operated without them. This meant that poor performance often went unnoticed. In such cases, FRAs were unable to exercise effective scrutiny on FRS and were largely incapable of holding FRS to account.

In terms of individuals sitting on FRAs, they had varying levels of expertise in FRS matters. Local councillors theoretically ought to draw on diverse backgrounds and experience to oversee FRSs, but in practice, their scrutiny and oversight of the services was questionable. In most cases, local councillors had limited experience of dealing with FRSs, either operationally or strategically. Their lack of experience and their other commitments resulted in an inadequate ability to robustly challenge their local FRSs. Local councillors often struggled to understand the fire and rescue environment, especially the day-to-day operational provision of services. Their insufficient understanding and knowledge of the fire sector resulted in regularly deferring to the Chief

Fire Officer (CFO) as a subject expert. In addition, CFOs formed bonds with local councillors, particularly chairs of FRAs, which ultimately contributed to distorted decision-making and limited scrutiny of local FRSs. Inexperienced local councillors preferred to rely on the CFOs' expertise rather than be accountable themselves for decision-making, which would have affected both the service and their political appointment (see Chapter 4).

The relationship between FRAs and FRSs was quite distant and formal. FRAs would meet quarterly on a formal basis with no further follow-up meetings, resulting in a relatively distant communication between FRAs and senior management. This was confirmed by senior managers who indicated that they felt accountable to their FRAs only when reporting on a formal basis. They argued that the more difficult the decisions they were asking the FRA to take, the more scrutiny and accountability from the FRA they got in return. For example, one CFO indicated that local councillors did hold them to account when taking decisions that could have costed the service a lot of money.

Accountability, and more specifically overview and scrutiny, within FRSs also cascaded down from governing bodies and management hierarchies to the front line. Perceptions on scrutiny and oversight differed between senior management staff and front-line staff. Firefighters theoretically perceived senior management as vertically accountable downwards to their staff because of their duty of care to their employees, including front-line firefighters and professional services staff (HR, finance, communications and IT). According to the firefighters, CFOs had the ultimate accountability for managing the FRS staff because of the nature of working in a hierarchical uniformed service with notions of rank (Andrews et al., 2014). CFOs were therefore ultimately responsible for anything that happened in the service. In practice, firefighters indicated that they were insufficiently informed about what was happening in the organisation. More specifically, they were often not informed about the decisions taken by senior management that ultimately had an impact on the front-line.

Notwithstanding the issues around inadequate communication down the hierarchy, firefighters felt accountable to both senior management and their direct line managers for their day-to-day responsibilities. At the same time, line managers were able to oversee their subordinates' performance and had an ability to reprimand them disciplinarily if they were underperforming. This reflects a bi-directional relationship, in which CFOs were accountable to the staff, and the staff perceived themselves as accountable to their line managers on the performance of delegated duties, and ultimately felt accountable to their CFO, as the leader of the organisation. Managers were bureaucratically accountable for supervising lower-level staff on the performance of delegated duties, and front-line staff felt downward bureaucratic accountability because of the duty of care from their senior management. The bureaucratic command–control relationship was therefore exemplified under this type of accountability.

It is noticeable that front-line officers felt there was an adequate level of scrutiny within FRSs, for example through a bi-directional accountability relationship between firefighters and their line managers. Nevertheless, FRSs generally perceived that FRAs provided an inadequate level of scrutiny on their performance. The issues around inadequate FRA members' knowledge, overreliance on the chief's expertise, lack of independent scrutiny committees as well as other councillors' commitments were the main factors that had contributed to the poor FRA scrutiny and oversight over FRSs. As a result, FRAs were unable to exercise their statutory role effectively and were largely incapable of holding FRSs to account.

Performance Management

Before 2010, FRSs were bureaucratically accountable for performance to the Audit Commission. The Audit Commission carried out corporate and service inspections until it was abolished between 2010 and 2015. This included external audit as well as financial and non-financial performance assessments of FRSs. If performing inadequately, FRSs were subject to potential consequences, including government intervention (see Chapter 5). The Audit Commission assessments were criticised by government and some local authorities for being 'top-down, costly, not providing significant "added-value" and focussing upon corporate processes rather than operational performance' (Downe et al., 2018, p. 61). Many condemned its performance measurement and target-setting approach, and the Audit Commission was abolished in 2010.

> *The original inspections [pre-2005 by Her Majesty's Fire Service Inspectorate] were … just like some an old boys' club… the actual testing the efficiency and effectiveness of the Fire and Rescue Services was just a pantomime really. Then came the Audit Commission… everything had a target to the point that you lost the point of doing it. And again, that was a sort of show-boating exercise where people tried to satisfy the metric. (Area Manager 1, Case Study 4)*

External performance management was significantly diminished following the abolition of the Audit Commission. Between 2010 and 2017, FRSs became responsible for managing their own performance as result of the

Coalition Government's policies of austerity-localism (Lowndes & Pratchett, 2012) and sector-led improvement (Murphy & Ferry, 2018). Senior managers argued that they were ultimately accountable for performance (or potential lack of performance) in their organisations under sector-led improvement. They were responsible for setting performance measures in service delivery plans and potential progress against the predefined targets in their services.

Accountability for performance also cascaded down to the firefighter level. Front-line staff felt accountable for the delivery of the predefined performance targets such as response times. Every aspect of a firefighter's job was recorded, including response times, the amount of prevention and protection work, the number of smoke alarms fitted and the provision of education. Firefighters were accountable to their line managers for how they operationally perform, whether it was response to emergencies or carrying out prevention work.

FRSs were ultimately accountable to their local FRAs for meeting performance targets. This is because FRAs were responsible for monitoring FRSs' work and ultimately ensuring that they meet the organisation's goals in an effective and efficient manner. Senior managers were responsible for setting the detailed targets and tracking the front-line staff's performance, while front-line staff were implementing the predefined targets in their day-to-day provision of services.

Horizontal Accountability

Horizontal accountability is a form of accountability between parties operating or collaborating in the same areas of interest. Typically, all parties are equal to one another, and more negotiation and collaboration than vertical command takes place under this direction of accountability. Horizontal accountability occurs with other emergency services working towards public safety, but it could also be observed at a team level within the service when responding to incidents. This could also be the case when two or more FRSs respond to large incidents. In the next subsection, external and internal collaboration is discussed in more detail.

External and Internal Collaboration

Before the Policing and Crime Act 2017, FRSs were involved in external collaboration exercises with other emergency services, key stakeholders and other partners. However, there was no statutory legal duty imposed on FRSs to work collaboratively with other emergency services. This meant that FRSs theoretically were not in a horizontal bureaucratic accountability relationship with any partners at the time, because none of the collaboration exercises introduced before 2017 were closely supervised, and there were no clearly stated rules for these collaborations. Although collaboration and partnership working had been enabled and encouraged by the Local Government Act 1999, Civil Contingencies Act 2004 and Crime and Disorder Act 1998, FRSs were not mandated to collaboratively respond to them with other partners (although they could have been criticised in post-incident inquiries and coroner's courts, most notably after the Manchester Arena Terrorist Attack) (Kerslake, 2018; Saunders, 2021, 2022, 2023).

However, bureaucratic accountability was prevalent when working in teams within FRSs. All fire and rescue staff have been working towards the same goal – public safety. Team working, mutual dependence and team culture were features of fire services, since members of the team (known as the 'watch') were highly dependent on each other, particularly when responding to incidents and dangerous contexts. Participants, particularly in the focus groups, highlighted that they were accountable for their own actions to their colleagues and senior officers, and vice versa. However, front-line staff, when working in a team, also acted as subordinates, as they were bureaucratically accountable to their superiors for the performance of delegated duties. This meant that they felt bureaucratically accountable for their team response to their watch managers, who were then accountable up to the senior management. Firefighters at the front-line worked together, shared information and negotiated how to approach each incident, although there was always a single incident commander involved, who was responsible for the whole incident (Wilsher, 2019). Although primarily associated with a strong hierarchy and ranks, FRSs also exhibited a strong horizontal accountability team culture to their managers and to the public. Although horizontal accountability was important when team working, firefighters also pointed out a blame culture could exist at the front-line. Making a wrong decision meant that firefighters could bear some consequences, primarily from their line managers. Making incorrect decisions and learning from the decisions made was therefore highlighted as an issue requiring greater attention from middle and senior management.

Diagonal Accountability

Diagonal accountability relationships are in between hierarchical and horizontal forms of accountability. They are the kind of relationships in which there are no powers to enforce compliance; however, the consequences still might be severe (Schillemans, 2008). Inspection bodies and audit institutions are examples of diagonal accountability relationships, in which FRSs have been involved over the decades. In this subsection, inspections and peer review are discussed in more detail.

Inspections and Peer Review

Before the Policing and Crime Act 2017, FRSs were diagonally accountable to His/Her Majesty's Fire Service Inspectorate (HMFSI) until 2007. HMFSI was superseded by the Audit Commission, who had been collecting performance information on FRSs since its establishment in 1983 (Campbell-Smith, 2008). Following HMFSI's formation in 1947, the inspectorate monitored the standards and operational performance of FRSs by providing advice on standards and compliance. However, the inspectorate did not hold FRSs bureaucratically to account for performance, as its role was primarily to provide the sector with fire standards. This meant that the level of scrutiny on FRSs' performance was limited. The HMFSI closed in 2007, by which time the role of external inspection had already passed on to the Audit Commission. However, after 2010, the Audit Commission no longer undertook inspections, and the Commission was gradually wound down before being formally closed in 2015.

FRSs became subject to a new sector-led improvement regime, which replaced the inspectorate and the Audit Commission (see Downe et al., 2018; Murphy & Ferry, 2018). Sector-led improvement involved moving accountability from the national level and placing responsibilities in the hands of local FRAs, by giving them more flexibility and freedom to deliver local services. Peer review was one of the main initiatives of the sector-led improvement regime. Fire peer challenge and operational assessments were co-ordinated by the Local Government Association (LGA) and involved senior staff from other FRS assessing their peer service. There were also thematic reviews of certain areas of business.

> *A team of people from across the sector would land in an organisation and basically do like an HMI inspection…I can understand the allegations or accusations of it being quite weak because it wasn't quite marking your own homework, but it was quite friendly! (Director of Prevention and Protection, Case Study 5)*

Senior managers indicated that this form of diagonal bureaucratic accountability was weak, as it was more of a friendly visit than an assessment done by an independent body. Furthermore, the results of peer challenges were not transparent as they were only shared internally. Front-line staff did not express their views on previous arrangements under this type of accountability, as they were not familiar with them. Further investigation of the impact of sector-led improvement regime is discussed in Chapter 6 of this book.

The next section of this chapter moves on to explain the FRSs' perceptions of bureaucratic accountability within vertical, horizontal and diagonal dimensions after the introduction of the provisions of the Policing and Crime Act 2017.

ACCOUNTABILITY ARRANGEMENTS AFTER THE POLICING AND CRIME ACT 2017

Vertical Accountability

The Policing and Crime Act 2017 introduced alternative governance arrangements for FRSs, including the Police, Fire and Crime Commissioner (PFCC) governance model, replacing FRAs, the establishment of an external inspectorate for all FRSs and greater collaboration between the emergency services. This section discusses the understandings of vertical bureaucratic accountability under the sub-themes of overview and scrutiny, and performance management, in the long-standing FRA governance model (the representation model) and the PFCC governance model (the governance model) following the implementation of the Policing and Crime Act 2017.

Overview and Scrutiny

The UK government envisaged the governance and accountability regime in the fire sector to gradually change from the FRA governance model towards the PFCC governance model (May, 2016). However, since the introduction of the Policing and Crime Act 2017, most FRSs remained under the traditional FRA governance model. FRA-governed services have implemented various internal governance arrangements, including designated sub-committees, to improve scrutiny and oversight within all FRSs. Nonetheless, the majority of FRSs claimed the FRA arrangements remained largely inadequate in terms of scrutiny following the introduction of the Policing and Crime Act 2017. They identified various scrutiny deficiencies within their services and attempted to seek appropriate solutions to these problems. This, inter alia, involved revising their schemes of delegations to improve scrutiny and overview within their services. This, in fact, made FRSs feel more bureaucratically accountable for their duties to the FRAs as they were more familiar with the scope of their accountabilities within the service.

Two out of the three traditional FRA-governed services examined in this book (Case Study 1 and 2) adopted the 'representation' model of the Policing and Crime Act 2017. This meant that FRAs were able to appoint additional members to their boards, including a Police and Crime Commissioner (PCC) or a PCC representative. According to participants, the presence of the PCC or the PCC representative brought an outside perspective to the decision-making process. Having an additional individual, experienced in overseeing police services on the FRA, has brought more emergency services-specific bureaucratic accountability to their FRS. The influence of the PCC or the PCC representative was evident through questioning senior managers' decisions in FRA meetings. In those services where a PCC representative sat on the FRA, the PCC representative ensured that there was more challenge in FRA meetings and that information and the agenda were driven by the PCC through discussing the delivery and translation of the FRA strategy into operational plans within FRSs. The presence of the PCC or the PCC representative on the FRA therefore contributed to increased bureaucratic scrutiny within FRSs. Front-line staff were not directly affected by the 'representation' model changes and did not identify major changes with regards to the scrutiny and oversight of their day-to-day operational jobs and targets.

The Policing and Crime Act 2017 has also introduced a single-person fire authority to oversee local FRSs under the PFCC governance model. The PFCC's powers specifically include implementing a fire and rescue plan, setting fire and rescue service budgets and appointing and dismissing a CFO. The PFCC's role is therefore similar to the FRA's role. While FRAs consist of a group of local councillors overseeing the fire service, a PFCC is a single individual responsible for holding the fire service to account. Senior managers, from services that had transferred to the PFCC governance model, were unanimous in the view that the PFCC model brought an additional level of scrutiny when questioning the service's decisions:

> *I think the PFCC and the people that work with them have a much better understanding of the actual work we do in communities, so*

> *they are able to ask us the right questions. (Partnerships Manager, Case Study 4)*

> *We now have a commissioner that is very, very focused, switched on, asked some very difficult and awkward questions. (DCFO, Case Study 6)*

Senior management found PFCCs to be bureaucratically holding fire services to account. They indicated that the depth and detail of scrutiny improved as a result of having a PFCC overseeing the service. Senior managers argued that PFCCs and the PFCC's support staff had both the experience of working with communities, as well as knowledge of policing, which ultimately contributed to better understanding of emergency services governance and increased scrutiny from PFCCs. In addition, the actions and decisions of PFCCs were also scrutinised by local Police, Fire and Crime Panels. Their role included reviewing the PFCC's plans and annual reports, confirming senior appointments and vetoing the PFCC's proposed precept.

By attempting to bring FRSs into greater collaboration with police services through the PFCC model of governance, the Policing and Crime Act 2017 highlighted the differences between fire and police in terms of clear operational independence for their Chief Officers. In contrast to Chief Constables, CFOs under the PFCC governance model had no operational independence. In all cases of the PFCC governance model (Case Studies 4, 5 and 6), interviewees highlighted tensions between their CFO and their PFCC. This is because PFCCs had too much operational power over FRSs, while CFOs had insufficient operational responsibilities and independence. This created a considerable tension and real interference in operational issues with the single-person leadership, which on occasions led to conflicts between CFOs and PFCCs, when the goals of PFCCs diverged from those of CFOs. Some senior managers recognised that having a single-person governing body instead of a group of individuals contributed to potential conflicts, especially if there was a personality clash between the PFCC and the CFO. Despite the PFCCs' experience of working in communities and within policing, senior managers indicated that PFCCs did not comprehend the operational side of FRSs and ultimately should not be responsible for operational decision-making. In all cases (in both PFCC- and FRA-governed services), senior management highlighted the need for reform in the fire sector, which would provide clarity in the divide between strategic and operational issues. They argued for CFOs to be responsible for the operational side of FRSs, while PFCCs remain in charge of the service's strategy. Despite concerns about limited operational independence, senior managers noted that decision-making under the PFCC governance model became faster and more structured. They attributed this improvement to streamlined oversight by a single PFCC, which eliminated layers of FRA bureaucracy.

In terms of the front line, staff were generally aware of the governance changes within their service. However, they were not familiar with how the governance changes might have changed the scrutiny of their activities. They still felt ultimately accountable to their CFO rather than a politician overseeing their service. Watch managers indicated that the introduction of new governance structures enabled greater scrutiny at lower levels of directorate boards than before the Policing and Crime Act 2017. This was mainly because of the involvement of the PFCC's support staff at lower levels within the service. Nonetheless, front-line staff continued to perceive their accountability demands largely in the same way as before the introduction of the Policing and Crime Act 2017.

As a result of the Policing and Crime Act 2017, bureaucratic accountability has remained primarily about FRSs' responsibility to report to and be scrutinised by a governing body, which oversees the service's organisational strategy. The findings show that the arrangements brought in by the Policing and Crime Act 2017, including both the reformed FRA as well as the PFCCs, have clarified and improved sources of scrutiny and accountability. Under both governance models, scrutiny became more structured and systematic through the PCC representation or PFCC oversight over the service.

Performance Management

Since the introduction of the Policing and Crime Act 2017, performance has continued to be scrutinised internally and vertically, either by an FRA or by a PFCC. External performance management was re-introduced through the creation of the inspectorate, His Majesty's Inspectorate of Constabulary and Fire & Rescue Services (HMICFRS), which holds FRSs accountable.

Having a PCC or a PCC representative present on an FRA has increased pressure on FRSs to improve their performance. FRSs that remained under the FRA governance arrangements were also concerned about a potential 'takeover' if their service was underperforming:

> *By having that extra pressure that if the authority and the organisation don't perform, then there is the possibility that the PCC would be driven to take over or to put a bid in to take over,*

> *to put forward a business case. Whereas before the legislation, there was nothing really challenging the FRAs. (Area Manager 2, Case Study 1)*

FRSs were aware of the possibility of a PCC 'takeover' if underperforming and therefore felt that they had to adequately perform under their FRA. Interviewees viewed a potential takeover as a threat. CFOs, together with other senior managers, were therefore mindful of building an effective rapport with their PCCs, in case of a sudden business case submission from their PCCs. The threat of a potential governance change was also pointed out by the front-line staff.

> *Certainly, my perception is if you are not performing as a Fire and Rescue Service then we will hit you with a big stick of the PCC and potentially you'll be taken over. (Firefighter, Case Study 1)*

Having a PCC or a PCC representative sitting on an FRA generally made the fire services more conscious of building an effective relationship with PCCs or PCC representatives in case of a potential change of governance to the PFCC model, as indicated by both senior managers and front-line staff. FRSs generally felt greater bureaucratic performance-oriented accountability under the reformed FRA rather than under the previous arrangement.

New channels of communication up to the PFCCs were identified in all three services that had transferred to the PFCC model of governance. They included establishment of specific internal performance-oriented boards focused on performance management. These accountability structures contributed to increased scrutiny within their service, primarily because of the detail and depth of conversations around performance management. Senior managers attributed this enhanced scrutiny to the PFCCs and their office staff, who had experience of analysing performance within policing. Nonetheless, some found the arrangements, in particular the meetings, as too bureaucratic. Senior managers were initially hopeful that the new arrangements would reduce the bureaucratic burden on FRSs. Instead, they found that the performance-oriented arrangements contributed to greater demand in terms of scrutiny and accountability for senior officers. Having too many senior leadership meetings was argued to be counterproductive in delivering accountability, as the meetings were perceived as excessively bureaucratic. Reducing the frequency of meetings was proposed as a solution to less bureaucratic arrangements under the PFCC governance model.

Overall, in both governance models, participants found an increased focused on performance management. In FRA-governed services, staff were conscious of a potential takeover bid from a PCC if inadequately performing. In PFCC-governed services, FRSs felt that the new performance-oriented arrangements increased the focus on performance, but also were heavily bureaucratic and created unnecessary burden on services. Notwithstanding the difficulties, FRSs felt more accountable for performance management to their governing bodies since the introduction of the Policing and Crime Act 2017.

Horizontal Accountability

Horizontal accountability continued to be operationalised primarily as a mechanism for collaboration between agencies responsible for public safety. Since the introduction of the Policing and Crime Act 2017, this form of accountability has been formalised, requiring structured engagement with other emergency services. This section explains how horizontal bureaucratic accountability has been operationalised since the introduction of the 2017 legislation in FRSs.

External and Internal Collaboration

The Policing and Crime Act 2017 formalised the duty on emergency services to collaborate, where it is in the interests of their efficiency or effectiveness and attempted to accelerate it into other areas. This meant that FRSs, together with other emergency services, have become bureaucratically accountable for service collaboration, which had not been the case before the introduction of the Policing and Crime Act 2017. The evidence shows that the vast majority of collaborative activities (excluding those relating to the COVID-19 pandemic) has been between police and fire services in both FRA-governed and PFCC-governed services. The Policing and Crime Act 2017 established closer working relationship between the two services, and in the case of PFCC-governed services, launched joint decision-making with the police. This meant that police forces and FRSs ultimately worked towards the same goal, which is community safety. In those services that adopted the PFCC model of governance, having clear goals established together with the police contributed to closer collaborative working. Interviewees found that CFOs and Chief Constables had formed close accountability relationships when working under the PFCC governance model. Chiefs provided constructive feedback to one another and aimed to focus on services' learning and improvement. Other examples of collaboration initiatives included joint first responders work, road safety campaigns, back-office support and sharing estates initiatives. The duty to collaborate created a focus for FRSs (and the police) to explore all possible approaches to collaboration.

While FRSs identified a number of ways to collaborate with the police, FRSs reported limited collaboration with ambulance services. The majority of FRA-governed services argued that it was not possible to be accountable to other emergency services, as they had different governance arrangements than FRSs:

> *We've got a close relationship [with ambulance services] but not from an accountability point of view...my relationship with the chief constable now is stronger than it ever has been... but I wouldn't say it's one of accountability, we don't hold each other to account, other than in a professional standard as kind of professional peers. (CFO, Case Study 1)*

Senior managers from FRA-governed services agreed that there was no scrutiny relationship between fire services and other emergency services due to different governance arrangements. Nonetheless, the 2017 legislation enabled all services, including those that remained under the FRA arrangements, to work together as professional peers in responding collaboratively to incidents (see Chapter 6). Bureaucratic accountability also continued when working internally within FRSs.

Overall, FRSs remained horizontally bureaucratically accountable for internal collaboration within the fire service. Since 2017, they have also been theoretically involved in an external horizontal accountability relationship with two other emergency services, namely the police and ambulance services. In practice, in PFCC-governed services, FRSs viewed their relationship with the police as one of mutual accountability, while those under FRA governance did not, primarily due to differences in governance arrangements between the two services. FRSs also felt that there was very limited horizontal accountability relationship between ambulance services and fire services under both governance models.

Diagonal Accountability

Diagonal accountability relationships, as previously stated, are usually developed with inspection bodies and external audit institutions. Following the Policing and Crime Act 2017, these relationships have changed for all FRSs, primarily due to the establishment of HMICFRS. The following section explains in detail how diagonal bureaucratic accountability has been operationalised since 2017 in the fire sector.

Inspections

HMICFRS's role has been to provide assurance on how effective and efficient FRSs are, how well they manage their people and whether they are fulfilling their statutory obligations to improve performance as well as accountability. The inspectorate's function has therefore been to bureaucratically hold FRSs to account for performance and report its findings in public reports. However, HMICFRS have been unable to sanction FRSs for poor performance due to diagonal accountability relationship in which there are no powers to enforce compliance; however, the consequences still might be severe. FRSs viewed the establishment of the inspectorate as an additional method of scrutiny. The inspectorate's role is to assess each service's effectiveness, efficiency, and its people, and the inspection outcome, in a form of a publicly available report, summarises whether the service has delivered what it had originally set out to deliver or not. It also recommends areas for improvement and learning for each service.

The results of the inspection process have been available to all the FRAs and all the PFCCs who subsequently scrutinise the service's performance based on the HMICFRS reports. In both governance models, participants argued that inspection reports helped FRAs and PFCCs to scrutinise their FRSs, as the reports clearly showed which areas required improvement. This often simplified the governing bodies' overview and scrutiny responsibilities by having ready reports to assess their service's performance.

Although perceptions on the inspectorate were mainly positive, there were also views that the inspection process was a siloed tick-box exercise focused on compliance rather than improvement. For example, when looking at certain areas of FRSs' responsibilities, the actual level and depth of activities was not investigated, which ultimately resulted in focusing on quantity over quality. Nonetheless, services were required to prepare '*to make sure everyone looks tidy…make sure it's perfect*' (Watch Manager 2, Case Study 2). Under both governance models, senior managers and front-line staff identified burdensome requirements of the inspection process. This was because HMICFRS has placed requirements upon the fire services with regard to the amount of information they are required to prepare ahead of an inspection visit.

> *When people start imposing targets... I think that the quality goes out of the work and it's all down to quantity, we've got to hit this, we've got to hit that, and a lot of the quality disappears. (Firefighter, Case Study 1)*

> *There is a lot of paperwork, there's a lot of red tape and there's a lot of preparation involved in making sure that when the inspection takes place, all the information's available for the inspectorate. (Director of Finance, Case Study 5)*

The burdensome requirements were mainly expressed in relation to preparing for the inspection visit by putting together data and information. This involved extra services' capacity, taking the staff's time away from their day-to-day responsibilities.

Overall, many senior managers believed that the inspection process brought bureaucratic scrutiny back into the fire sector. However, staff at both senior management and front-line levels indicated that the inspection process introduced burdensome requirements into their services, including preparing in advance for inspection visits, ultimately creating accountability overloads. The latter was perceived as superficial by many participants as it did not show the 'real' state of FRSs, which could have been actioned through unannounced visits.

CONCLUSION

This chapter has reviewed FRSs' understandings of bureaucratic accountability before and after the introduction of the Policing and Crime Act 2017. Table 3 summarises FRSs' bureaucratic accountability understandings in relation to vertical, horizontal and diagonal directions.

FRSs before the introduction of the Policing and Crime Act 2017 were vertically bureaucratically accountable to FRAs as they had responsibility for the leadership, strategic direction, scrutiny and oversight of the services. However, they found the FRA scrutiny arrangements as largely limited due to the lack of an in-depth understanding of fire operational and strategic matters, which ultimately contributed to poor scrutiny and oversight over FRSs, and ultimately less clear accountability. In addition, slow and bureaucratic decision-making and excessive focus on formal engagements held by FRAs were counterproductive in holding the services to account.

Table 3. Fire and Rescue Services' Understandings of Bureaucratic Accountability Before and After the Introduction of the Policing and Crime Act 2017.

		Before the 2017 Act	After the 2017 Act	
Directions	**Main Sub-Themes**	**FRA-Governed Services**	**FRA-Governed Services**	**PFCC-Governed Services**
Vertical (governing body – fire and rescue service, senior managers – front line staff)	Overview and scrutiny	*Limited* scrutiny from an FRA.	*Moderate* scrutiny as a result of the PCC sitting on an FRA.	*Extensive* scrutiny as a result of the PFCC.
	Performance management	*Moderate* accountability from top to bottom through meeting performance targets.	*Moderate* accountability as a result of the PCC sitting on an FRA.	*Extensive* accountability through performance-oriented structures within services.
Horizontal (fire and rescue service – other emergency services; fire and rescue service staff)	External and internal collaboration	*Limited* accountability relationship when collaborating with police and ambulance services. *Extensive* accountability within services when working in teams.	*Limited* accountability relationship when collaborating with police and ambulance services. *Extensive* accountability within services when working in internal teams.	*Moderate* accountability relationship when collaborating with police. *Limited* accountability relationship when collaborating with ambulance services. *Extensive* accountability within services when working in internal teams.
Diagonal (inspectorates/ peers – fire and rescue service)	Inspections and peer review	*Limited* accountability towards inspection bodies or peer organisations.	*Extensive* bureaucratic scrutiny on services focused on performance.	*Extensive* bureaucratic scrutiny on services focused on performance.

Source: Author's interpretation.

The introduction of the Policing and Crime Act 2017 brought new overview and scrutiny arrangements under the reformed FRA governance model and the PFCC governance model. In the reformed FRA governance model, the staff found improving scrutiny as a result of the optional PCC or PCC representative presence and oversight on an FRA. In the PFCC governance model, the depth and detail of scrutiny, as well as the speed of decision-making, also improved as a result of having a single individual overseeing the service. PFCCs effectively utilised their understanding, knowledge and experience of policing in the fire and rescue context. Consequently, they effectively scrutinised the decisions. Although, on occasions, they had too much operational power when taking decisions against the advice of professional CFOs. Before the 2017 legislation, services were also vertically accountable for meeting performance targets internally within their services. The 2017 Act increased pressure on services to improve performance. In the case of reformed FRA-governed services, participants feared that if they were underperforming, they could be taken over by a PCC. In PFCC-governed services, newly established performance-oriented structures resulted in increased accountability within services.

FRSs before the 2017 legislation did not feel horizontally bureaucratically accountable to other organisations (other than when acting in major emergencies). At the time, there was no statutory legal duty imposed on FRSs to collaborate with their partners. The Policing and Crime Act 2017 introduced a formal duty to externally collaborate with other emergency services, which officially required FRSs to collaborate with police and ambulance services. Under the FRA governance model, FRSs did not perceive the relationship with either of the two services to have an accountability element due to different governance arrangements. On the other hand, FRSs under the PFCC governance model established closer working arrangements with the police services as result of being scrutinised by the same individual. Consequently, they felt more bureaucratically accountable to police horizontally, in that the services were working towards the same goal, which is public safety, and providing constructive feedback to each other to find the best options of service delivery to the public. Notably, they did not identify the relationship with ambulance services as one of accountability due to different governance arrangements. This demonstrates that the 2017 legislation has changed how FRSs perceive horizontal accountability. Nonetheless, FRSs before and after the 2017 legislation continued to feel horizontally accountable when working in teams within their services, as they were held bureaucratically accountable by their line managers.

Before the introduction of the Policing and Crime Act 2017, there was limited diagonal bureaucratic accountability within FRSs. FRSs were accountable to HMFSI, which was subsequently superseded by the Audit Commission, before inspections were abolished in 2010. FRSs became subject to the sector-led improvement regime that proved to be a weak source of bureaucratic accountability. The 2017 legislation established HMICFRS, which provided bureaucratic scrutiny on services and focused on their performance. FRSs started to feel bureaucratically accountable to the inspectorate under both FRA and PFCC governance models. However, they indicated that the inspection process had introduced some burdensome bureaucratic requirements into their services, which could ultimately create accountability overloads.

Overall, FRSs changed how they understand bureaucratic accountability in all three dimensions (vertical, horizontal and diagonal) as a result of the introduction of the Policing and Crime Act 2017. More specifically, they felt greater bureaucratic accountability at various levels under both governance models as a result of the 2017 legislation.

REFERENCES

Andrews, R., Ashworth, R., & Meier, K. J. (2014). Representative bureaucracy and fire service performance. *International Public Management Journal*, *17*(1), 1–24.

Bovens, M. (2007). Analysing and assessing accountability: A conceptual framework. *European Law Journal*, *13*(4), 447–468.

Campbell-Smith, D. (2008). *Follow the money: The Audit Commission public money and the management of public services 1983–2008*. Allen Lane.

Downe, J., Martin, S., & Doering, H. (2018). Peer challenge: A sector-led approach to performance improvement in fire and rescue services. In P. Murphy & K. Greenhalgh (Eds.), *Fire and rescue services: Leadership and management perspectives* (pp. 61–75). Springer.

Kerslake, R. (2018). *The Kerslake report: An independent review into the preparedness for, and emergency response to, the Manchester Arena attack on 22nd May 2017*. TSO.

Lowndes, V., & Pratchett, L. (2012). Local governance under the coalition government: Austerity, localism and the 'Big Society'. *Local Government Studies*, *38*(1), 21–40.

May, T. (2016, May 14). *Home Secretary speech on fire reform*. https://www.gov.uk/government/speeches/home-secretary-speech-on-fire-reform

Mulgan, R. (2003). *Holding power to account: Accountability in modern democracies*. Palgrave Macmillan.

Murphy, P., & Ferry, L. (2018). Another turn of the screw: Fire and rescue under the Coalition Government of 2010–2015. In P. Murphy & K. Greenhalgh (Eds.), *Fire and rescue services: Leadership and management perspectives* (pp. 45–59). Springer.

Romzek, B. (2000). Dynamics of public accountability in the era of reform. *International Review of Administrative Sciences*, *66*(1), 21–44.

Romzek, B. S., & Dubnick, M. J. (1987). Accountability in the public sector: Lessons from the Challenger tragedy. *Public Administration Review*, *47*(3), 227–238.

Saunders, J. (2021). *Manchester Arena Inquiry: Volume 1: Security for the Arena*. https://www.gov.uk/government/publications/manchester-arena-inquiry-volume-1-security-for-the-arena

Saunders, J. (2022). *Manchester Arena Inquiry: Volume 2: Emergency response*. https://www.gov.uk/government/publications/manchester-arena-inquiry-volume-2-emergency-response

Saunders, J. (2023). *Manchester Arena Inquiry: Volume 3: Radicalisation and preventability*. https://www.gov.uk/government/publications/manchester-arena-inquiry-volume-3-radicalisation-and-preventability

Schillemans, T. (2008). Accountability in the shadow of hierarchy: The horizontal accountability of agencies. *Public Organization Review*, *8*, 175–194.

Sinclair, A. (1995). The chameleon of accountability: Forms and discourses. *Accounting, Organizations and Society*, *20*(2), 219–237.

Willems, T., & Van Dooren, W. (2011). Lost in diffusion? How collaborative arrangements lead to an accountability paradox. *International Review of Administrative Sciences*, *77*(3), 505–530.

Wilsher, R. (2019). Personal reflections on fire and rescue incident command. In P. Wankhade, L. McCann, & P. Murphy (Eds.), *Critical perspectives on the management and organization of emergency services* (pp. 52–69). Routledge.

4

FINDINGS: POLITICAL ACCOUNTABILITY

ABSTRACT

This chapter examines the dynamics of political accountability within English Fire and Rescue Services (FRSs) before and after the governance reforms introduced by the Policing and Crime Act 2017. Using Romzek and Dubnick's (1987) framework, it explores vertical, horizontal and diagonal accountability relationships and their changes under two governance models: Fire and Rescue Authorities (FRAs) and Police, Fire and Crime Commissioners (PFCCs). Findings reveal that pre-2017 FRA arrangements offered indirect accountability through local councillors sitting on FRAs, while post-2017 reforms introduced direct electoral accountability in PFCC-governed services via PFCCs. However, the PFCC model also created more politicisation and short-term decision-making, often influenced by election cycles and party affiliations. Public engagement remained low under both models, though PFCC governance provided more opportunities but reduced transparency. Horizontal accountability primarily relied on personal relationships between officers and politicians, while diagonal accountability reflected influence from political parties and representative bodies. Overall, reforms enhanced political accountability, but political or individual priorities continued to be a distortion of FRSs' accountability in both governance models.

Keywords: Political accountability; Fire and Rescue Services; governance reform; public administration; directions of accountability

INTRODUCTION

Following the analysis of bureaucratic accountability relationships in Chapter 3, this book now focuses on the dynamics of political accountability in English Fire and Rescue Services (FRSs), where perceptions of accountability change as a result of governance reforms introduced by the Policing and Crime Act 2017. Political forms of accountability rely on responsiveness to the concerns of key stakeholders in representative democratic systems (Romzek & Dubnick, 1987). In a political accountability relationship, the representative makes decisions on behalf of the constituents, who can dismiss the representative(s) through elections. The representative might be an individual politician, for example an MP, a local councillor, a portfolio holder or a scrutiny chair, or representatives might embrace a group of politicians, for example, a sub-committee or board, which might or might not be politically balanced.

Political accountability requires FRSs to be responsive to their communities and their needs and ambitions. FRSs are accountable to their communities through their governing bodies who directly or indirectly elect them. This chapter describes FRSs' understandings of political accountability in relation to the vertical, horizontal and diagonal directions of accountability to address the '*accountability for what*' and '*accountability to whom*' dimensions of the conceptual framework, introduced in Chapter 2. More specifically, it examines how these understandings have changed in the context of the governance reforms brought in by the Policing and Crime Act 2017 (see Figs. 5 and 6).

ACCOUNTABILITY ARRANGEMENTS PRIOR TO THE POLICING AND CRIME ACT 2017

Vertical Accountability

In a vertical accountability relationship, a superior is calling for an account from those who are accountable (subordinate), including the rights to demand answers and to impose sanctions. Vertical accountability relationships feature direct vertical lines of command between a superior and a subordinate, with clear demands from the superior (Mulgan, 2003). This subsection covers the sub-themes of local elections and representation, decision-making, public engagement and transparency and responsiveness to communities, which

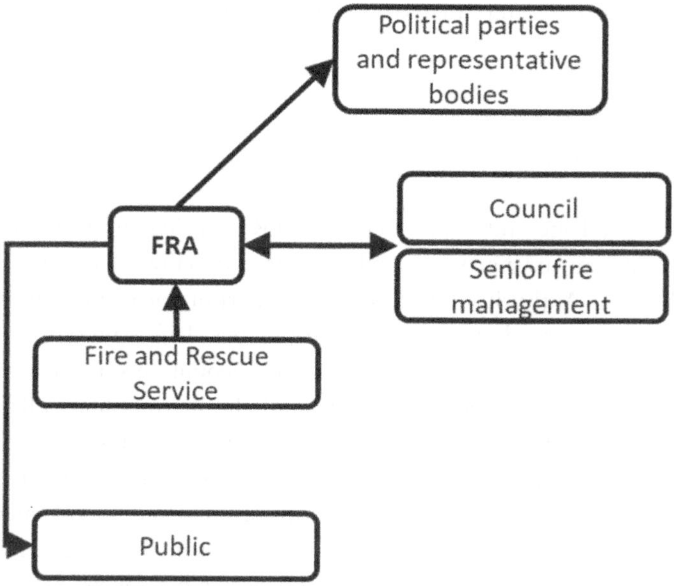

Source: Author's interpretation.

Fig. 5. Fire and Rescue Services' Understandings of Political Accountability Relationships in FRA-Governed Fire and Rescue Services Before the Introduction of the Policing and Crime Act 2017.

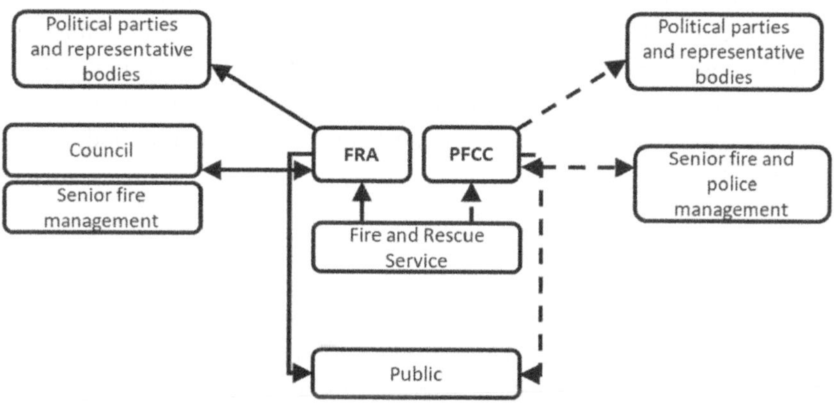

Fig. 6. Fire and Rescue Services' Understandings of Political Accountability Relationships in FRA-Governed (Solid Lines) and in PFCC-Governed (Dotted Lines) Fire and Rescue Services After the Introduction of the Policing and Crime Act 2017.

emerged from the data analysis on the vertical dimension of political accountability.

Local Elections and Representation

Prior to the Policing and Crime Act 2017, FRSs in England were all part of local government arrangements and were traditionally answerable to their Fire and Rescue Authority (FRA), which was part of one or more of the local councils that governed their administrative area. Different types of FRAs adopted different ways of holding FRSs to account through elected local councillors. Under the combined FRAs and the metropolitan FRAs, FRA members are drawn from councillors elected to local authorities, based on their size and political representation. They are appointed by their political group leaders to sit on an FRA. Under county council arrangements, the council is the FRA and all councillors attend full council meetings. However, the FRS has a single individual, a lead cabinet member for fire (also called a portfolio holder), who is appointed by the leader of the council, who makes a range of delegated decisions on FRSs.

Under all three types of FRA governance, the public were theoretically able to hold their FRA indirectly to account. The FRA governance model enabled local councillors to be directly elected by voters, albeit not directly elected to sit on an FRA (they were ultimately appointed by the political leaders). In practice, some senior managers (e.g., Chief Fire Officer (CFO), Case Study 4) found that the FRA arrangements did not provide political accountability because communities were not able to have their direct say on who sat on an FRA. In addition, residents had limited ability to dismiss FRA members. This in practice meant that communities had limited powers to hold individuals sitting on FRAs to account.

Decision-Making

Local councillors sitting on FRAs typically represented their political parties. The vast majority of councillors were members of political groups representing national and local political parties. A minority of local councillors were independent, and in some councils the independents formed a political group, although others chose to operate outside of any group or party affiliation. Senior managers and front-line staff believed that the FRA governance model facilitated constructive discussions and negotiations to take place between FRA members from different political parties. However, senior managers felt that decision-making processes were largely politically influenced. They pointed out a number of examples, when local councillors made decisions along party-political lines. For example, Labour-led FRAs had been influenced to a great extent by Trade Unions (with Labour affiliation). This, according to senior managers, meant that political affiliations ultimately had an impact on the delivery of services. This was seen to be exacerbated when a council majority was from the same political party as the central government in Westminster. The same party majority in both central government and the local FRA ultimately helped FRAs to take controversial decisions for FRSs. In the case when central government had a different party majority than the local FRA, the decision-making process could take considerably longer and was more complex, as the proposals from two different political parties would clash. Overall, decision-making on FRAs was easier when an FRA had a majority of local councillors from a single political party who agreed on certain matters.

Notwithstanding the political decision-making, FRAs seemed to be more politically accountable to local people than fire officers, as they had their final say on decisions taken in the service. This was also the case even if the decisions taken might not have been best for local people. Nonetheless, senior management observed that local councillors sitting on FRAs would not make any unpopular decisions with regards to the FRS immediately before local government elections.

> *They're very fearful of change because if they're in a political position, any change that affects their seat, they are very worried about... So if we say, we need to close that fire station because we're not getting value for money, if that's in a councillor's area and then the public say to them, well you're the lead councillor and you're allowing them to close a fire station, rather than them promoting the benefit that would come from closing that fire station, they then act against us and say, well actually it's really going to affect my seat in the next elections, so don't close that fire station, which actually is not the best thing to do in that area. (Area Manager 1, Case Study 3)*

On many occasions, FRA members were fearful of making any significant changes or taking controversial operational decisions in the run-up to elections because this would affect their chances of getting re-elected. Senior fire officers perceived local councillors' re-election as more important to local councillors than providing the public with value for money services. Party-political decision-making was detrimental to service delivery. The decisions made by FRAs often reflected political or individual priorities rather than benefits for local communities. According to senior officers, members of FRAs did not feel that residents can politically hold them to account, even though they were taking controversial operational decisions in the run up to elections. This is because the FRA governance model did not provide any direct mechanisms to hold them to account.

Public Engagement and Transparency

Before the Policing and Crime Act 2017, FRAs were required to have transparent processes in place to deliver accountability to the public and actively engage with local communities (DCLG, 2012). Local communities were therefore able to actively help to plan their local service delivery through effective consultation and involvement. For example, residents were able to participate in consultations on a local Integrated Risk Management Plan (IRMP), which was the basis of the service's strategy and ultimately the service's performance plan to create safer communities in the longer term.

In addition to the consultation exercises, FRAs were required to have arrangements in place to ensure that their decisions were open to public scrutiny. This was enabled by the FRA transparency mechanisms – the Local Accountability and Audit Act 2014 and the Local Government Transparency Code (DCLG, 2015). FRAs, like other English local authorities, had to publish many documents, including senior salaries, organisation charts and procurement information. FRAs also published papers and reports both before and after their meetings, which were open for public scrutiny. Each service had all the relevant FRA meeting data stored on its respective websites, open for public scrutiny. The public were able to access the data on their local service's websites, but, according to FRSs, the data were often insufficient on their own for residents to scrutinise their local service. FRA meetings were open for the public to attend and meet their local councillors. Residents were able to raise any issues concerning their local fire service. However, some senior managers suggested that these arrangements were not fit for purpose as they were not easily accessible to communities. They found online and more frequent meetings to be a better way of communicating relevant decisions made on FRAs to the public.

Nonetheless, residents were not particularly concerned about their FRSs' strategic matters because they had a lot of trust in the services, which ultimately meant that they did not wish to scrutinise some of their activities, or they trusted other key local stakeholders, such as local authorities, to act as 'proxy' scrutinisers. Engagement with fire services was notably lower than in sectors such as policing or healthcare, where issues tend to attract greater public attention. For most people, the priority was ensuring that emergency response worked when needed, and complaints were rare. Limited engagement was also linked to practical barriers, such as uncertainty about where to raise concerns or whom to contact within the service.

Overall, communities had a number of opportunities to engage with their local FRSs and the respective FRA. These included public consultations, attending FRA meetings and direct conversations with their local councillors. However, most residents did not actively engage in the detailed formal consultation processes of their local fire services, and most of the residents were not aware who has oversight of their service. In practice, the public were relatively unaware of how to hold their FRS to account or how to engage with the service.

Responsiveness to Communities

FRSs were responsive to communities through their FRAs. Each local councillor, as an elected member sitting on an FRA, represented their local communities' interest within the area in which they had been elected to serve their term of office. In many cases, senior management found that by representing the communities, local councillors were able to deal with the communities' issues at a local level.

> *They [FRA members] would have visited their local fire station, they would have got to know the crews, and they would have been aware of what's going on within their local area. So, the local community … if they'd got issues, they'd be able to go directly to their councillor, and their councillor could have come to the authority … they would have had contact with their local fire station, with officers, would have been able to … really deal with people's issues on a local level. (Director of Finance, Case Study 5)*

Senior managers understood that local councillors were often approached by their constituents about various issues, including FRSs, and they were able to bring them into the FRA meetings. This suggests that FRA members, although making decisions as local councillors, were actively involved in engaging and representing communities' needs and were ultimately politically accountable to their constituents.

Horizontal Accountability

In this subsection, horizontal political accountability relationships are discussed prior to the introduction of the Policing and Crime Act 2017. In comparison to vertical accountability, in horizontal accountability relationships, all parties are equal to one another, and more negotiation and collaboration than vertical command takes place. In FRSs' context, horizontal political accountability is operationalised in personal relationships between officers and politicians and focuses on providing constructive feedback.

Personal Relationships Between Officers and Politicians

FRSs and FRAs worked together not only on the basis of oversight and supervision (see Chapter 3) but also in the interest of local communities. Senior managers found relationships between officers and politicians to be crucial to working together and ultimately affecting the political decision-making within FRSs.

> *I see some county council FRSs doing extremely well. I think it's all to do with that relationship the CFO has with...potentially the lead of the county council, or the lead of a combined fire authority. (ACFO 2, Case Study 4)*

Although FRA members were overseeing senior managers' work, the relationship between them in this case was of a horizontal nature of mutual accountability as they both worked towards developing policies and strategies and had the same goal of maintaining effective service delivery. In particular, the relationship between CFOs and leaders of FRAs was important to providing effective leadership of FRSs on behalf of the public. Senior officers and politicians were ultimately acting in the best interest of communities when working together. They held each other accountable when providing constructive feedback on proposed decisions for the services. Negotiations held between them ultimately aimed to facilitate learning and improvement, maintain effective service delivery and keep local communities safe.

Diagonal Accountability

Diagonal political accountability characterises the relationship between FRSs and FRAs on the one hand and a third party (such as a political party or representative body) on the other. In such relationships, the third party might be influencing FRA's decisions about FRSs, which ultimately affect residents or FRSs' staff.

Local and National Politics

Prior to 2017, decision-making within FRSs was often shaped by the political affiliations of local councillors who sat on FRAs. Local councillors represented different political parties, or they were independent, whether sitting as part of a formal independent 'group' or individually. Senior managers and front-line staff both considered that political party membership affected certain decisions within FRSs. Local councillors on many occasions voted along party lines on their FRAs and ultimately made decisions that chimed with their party's political policy or strategy. Senior fire officers were, however, not aware if local councillors had been instructed by politicians higher up the political party or simply felt that they should be voting according to political party lines. Under this type of accountability, there were no powers to enforce compliance; however, the consequences from political parties could have nevertheless been significant (ultimately local councillors could be expelled from their political party for voting against their party's manifesto).

Representative Bodies

Political accountability also operated diagonally between FRAs, FRSs and the employees' representative bodies. Representative bodies included unions, associations and/or professions representing groups of individuals within the fire sector. They are generally acknowledged in accredited collective bargaining arrangements over terms and conditions of service. Their objectives are not always synonymous with the objectives of the governing body of the service. The evidence showed that the representative bodies, primarily trade unions, had a significant, but indirect, influence over the decisions undertaken by FRAs. This influence was often on long-term policy and strategy but could have also been on a particular issue or short-term decision.

FRSs are heavily unionised as a service. The Fire Brigades Union (FBU) is a trade union that represents the professional voice of firefighters. Front-line staff believed that their responsibilities were sometimes being taken too far away from their core duties, and the union's role is to protect firefighters' rights and the fundamental values of the service from any reforms that might jeopardise them. The FBU had a strong political influence on the service, as indicated by the interviewees. It would often put pressure on local FRAs to change decisions that might already have been made. In some cases, this led to national or local industrial disputes between the management, FRAs and the FBU (Case Study 2 and Case Study 6). In Case Study 2, the staff, represented by the union, successfully challenged decisions made by the CFO, ultimately persuading the FRA to reverse its original decision. CFOs did not have operational independence (see Chapter 3), meaning that they were not able to take operational decisions without FRA's approval. All decisions potentially had to go through FRAs. In this case, the Chief's decision was challenged by the unions on the FRA. The FBU was traditionally associated with the Labour Party, and the FRA in Case Study 2 also had a Labour majority. Subsequently, the individuals representing the Labour Party on the FRA helped to effect the ultimate change preferred by the unions. In Case Study 6, there was also a case that nearly led to industrial action. A proposed change was not introduced in a mutually acceptable manner and led to industrial issues between officers, the FRA and the FBU. This shows that the FBU as a representative body had an influence in affecting decisions in FRSs. This was particularly seen in the cases where the FRA had a Labour majority. Workforces, through their union representatives, challenged decisions taken by CFOs or FRAs, which led to the organisation taking a decision that chimed with union preferences. The representative bodies had no formal powers to enforce compliance on CFOs or FRAs; however, the potential consequences of union's action could have nevertheless been severe (for example, front-line staff going on strike).

The next section of this chapter moves on to explain the understandings of political accountability within vertical, horizontal and diagonal dimensions following the implementation of the Policing and Crime Act 2017.

ACCOUNTABILITY ARRANGEMENTS AFTER THE POLICING AND CRIME ACT 2017

Vertical Accountability

The Policing and Crime Act 2017 enabled FRSs to be taken over by a Police, Fire and Crime Commissioner (PFCC). The sections below describe the sub-themes that emerged from the analysis on the vertical dimension of political accountability in the traditional FRA governance model (the representation model) and in the PFCC governance model (the governance model), following the implementation of the Policing and Crime Act 2017.

Local Elections and Representation

In services that remained under the FRA governance model, the public continued to indirectly elect their local councillors sitting on an FRA. As a result of the 2017 legislation, Police and Crime Commissioner (PCC) or the PCC representative has been able to sit on an FRA. A PCC is directly elected by the local public in elections and is an additional politician among other local councillors appointed to sit on an FRA.

> *The PCC is just . . . another elected member. (Area Manager 2, Case Study 1)*

Senior managers perceived FRA members, including a PCC (or a PCC representative), as politicians elected by residents and subsequently appointed by council leaders to represent public interests. Indirect elections under the FRA governance model meant that local communities were not able to directly dismiss their FRA members (apart from the PCC); however, they were still responsible for electing individuals who could potentially sit on an FRA.

Since 2017, in services that adopted the PFCC governance model, residents have been able to elect an individual politician in PCC/PFCC elections in their area. The PFCC governance model has enabled local public to directly choose their preferred individual in charge of both policing and fire service. Senior managers found this way of electing the authority more accountable than the indirectly elected FRA arrangements.

> *One thing you can't argue is that it's less transparent and it's less accountable than what people have currently got because no fire authorities are elected to be fire authorities, people are elected to be councillors in councils, they are then appointed on to fire authorities. There is no [direct] electoral accountability in that whatsoever. . .if you don't like them [PFCC], you can get rid of them at the end of the day, and you can vote for somebody else. (CFO, Case Study 4)*

According to senior officers, the PFCC governance model provided direct political accountability to local communities, who were able to elect and dismiss their PFCC if they were not pleased with the politician overseeing their local fire service.

Decision-Making

The process of decision-making changed in both governance models as result of the introduction of the Policing and Crime Act 2017. In the FRA governance model, decision-making remained in the hands of FRA members who were local councillors. However, the 2017 Act has enabled a PCC or a PCC representative to sit on an FRA and directly influence the decision-making by having voting rights. Senior managers continued to believe that FRA governance arrangements enabled diverse conversations on certain matters during FRA meetings because of a number of individuals involved in decision-making who could step in and contribute to certain decisions. Nonetheless, they also agreed that the FRA governance model remained politically driven. Having a PCC or a PCC representative sitting on an FRA had no significant difference to the political nature of the strategic decision-making process as the individual was another politician representing their political party on an FRA. Senior managers found the presence of the PCC or the PCC representative as ultimately not affecting their final decision-making process. This is because local councillors outnumbered the individual PCC or the PCC representative, and the decision-making process remained heavily politically influenced. FRA members continued to vote in favour of their political party and often ignored the PCC's or the PCC representative's views. Decisions continued to be based upon political affiliations and potential impact on re-election, which meant that they were fairly cautious and 'conservative' in nature. On occasions, FRAs decided on operational matters in line with their party-political affiliations rather than advice focused upon effective service delivery. Senior managers agreed that politics should be kept separate from operational decision-making to ensure services are delivered effectively and in the best interests of local communities.

Firefighters were more concerned about the reformed 'representation' FRA model. They indicated that if a new PCC is elected, he or she could potentially change the political agenda on the FRA and ultimately take over their local FRS. In contrast to their senior officers, front-line staff believed that having a PCC or a PCC representative had meant changes to their FRAs. Front-line staff feared the unknown political consequences of being overseen by a different individual, whether it was a new PCC on the FRA or a PFCC. They were anxious about potential changes to the strategic vision for the service, which could affect the front-line staff as well as the senior managers and ultimately local communities.

In the PFCC governance model, the PFCC is ultimately responsible for decision-making. Senior managers claimed that having a single politician responsible for their FRS had brought 'short-termism' into the fire governance. Most senior managers noted that PFCCs, especially in the periods before the elections, would make populist decisions, which they thought would help PFCCs get re-elected. However, those decisions often had a detrimental impact on the local FRS and ultimately local communities. For example, some PFCCs decided not to increase the precept for the local taxpayers, which ultimately affected the service's capacities and capabilities. This reduced the quality of the service that the FRS provided to residents. On the other hand, it encouraged the public to vote for the existing PFCC to keep their local council tax at the same level as the year before. Decision-making under the PFCC governance model was therefore considered to be more influenced by the political election timetable.

> *As it gets closer to an election, the PFCC is looking for more and more good news to put in their press releases. And good news stories are fairly short lived obviously in political circles, you're only as good as your last headline at the end of the day, so they [PFCC] want to keep that going. (CFO, Case Study 4)*

> *Our commissioner won't make any unpopular decisions in the six months prior to an election period, which is a big frustration. So, you're working to a political timetable which is unhelpful. (Director of Prevention and Protection, Case Study 5)*

> *There are times when there is political involvement, which can be frustrating, particularly around the General Election time, we had some changes which we wanted to make, and it became very political ...it was very much motivated by the General Election and the involvement of local MPs. And once that had passed, the interest all disappeared from everybody. (DCFO, Case Study 6)*

Senior officers suggested that PFCCs take political decisions because they feel pressured by national and local political leaders. PFCCs, according to senior management, often felt that their governance position was largely due to their political affiliation, and they felt the need to reciprocate it through loyalty to the party-political line. This happened primarily around the

General Election time when PFCCs made certain decisions that did not harm the electoral chances of their party colleagues.

Having a single politician overseeing an FRS also means that the decision-making process can significantly change every time there is an election. A new individual from a different political party can come along with a new agenda for the service and change the direction in which it might be heading in the future. The possibility of a change in political agendas was perceived as a major concern for most senior managers who believed that political stability in the strategy and direction of FRSs was very important. In comparison, the FRA governance model was not significantly affected by the elections as the political composition of FRAs does not change as often as the individual politician.

Public Engagement and Transparency

One of the stated aims of the Policing and Crime Act 2017 was to enhance the accountability and transparency of the services to the public. FRSs have been required to provide transparency and accountability to their communities for their actions, as well as opportunities for communities to help to plan their local service development (Home Office, 2018). They have been legally obliged to provide such opportunities under both governance models.

FRSs that remained under the FRA arrangements continued to comply with the Local Authority Transparency Code 2015 and the Local Accountability and Audit Act 2014, as they did before the introduction of the Policing and Crime Act 2017 (see Chapter 5). The opportunities for communities to get involved in the development of their local service remained in place. Despite publishing required information, local communities were not particularly interested in directly scrutinising their local FRS. The 2017 Act has additionally enabled the communities to have their say on consultations when a PCC wishes to take over their local fire service. However, residents remained largely reluctant to be involved in the planning processes of their local FRS.

FRSs that experienced a transfer of governance to a PFCC have been required to comply with transparency requirements under Section 11 of the Police Reform and Social Responsibility Act 2011 and the Elected Local Policing Bodies (Specified Information) Order 2011, rather than the equivalent Local Government Acts. As with the FRA governance arrangements, these would include publishing senior officers' salaries, organisational charts, budgets, records of decisions taken and minutes of public meetings. However, this meant that the PFCC, or more precisely the Office of the PFCC, instead of an FRA, would publish the information and run public consultations under the PFCC model of governance. According to interviewees, this meant that more people have been able to get involved in the service's planning. Senior managers found that consultation response rates were higher under the PFCC governance model than under the FRA governance model. For example, under the PFCC governance model, communities were consulted on the potential increase of the precept for both policing and FRS in their local area, and the Fire and Rescue Plan, which sets out the service's strategic vision, priorities and objectives.

Residents have also been given other opportunities to actively take part in the services' decision-making processes under the PFCC governance structures. The quarterly FRA meetings have been replaced with monthly meetings, attended by a CFO, a PFCC and a Chief Constable and other senior managers. They have been live streamed online, and despite low public attendance, in some cases, the communities have had the opportunity to raise questions about their service. Senior fire officers felt that regular public meetings with the PFCC provided a source of accountability and transparency to residents. Accountability was evident in cases where the meetings facilitated interactions between the PFCC, the fire service and the members of the public. In cases, where interaction was not possible, they at least offered more transparency into the decision-making process.

Some services, however, experienced reduced levels of transparency in terms of publishing key or relevant documents. As previously stated, FRSs that transferred to the PFCC governance model have been required to comply with different transparency requirements, meaning that the Office of the PFCC has been responsible for publishing documents. In one case, senior manager found that transparency had reduced in comparison to the FRA governance model, as some information, including meeting minutes, was no longer published online before, during and after the decision-making process. Under the FRA governance model, items to be submitted for decision to the FRA were published in advance, alongside reports and recommendations, before the FRA made their decision and subsequently decisions were captured in the meeting minutes, which were published according to established timescales. Senior managers found this to be a transparent method of demonstrating to the public the available options and recommendations in meeting agendas before the final decisions of the FRA. Under the PFCC arrangements, decision notes were required to be published only after a decision was taken, clearly reducing transparency of decision-making and ultimately reducing residents' possibilities to actively hold the PFCC accountable for the decisions.

Responsiveness to Communities

FRSs have been responsive to communities either through an FRA or a PFCC. The FRA 'representation' model has allowed PCCs to sit on an FRA and have voting rights but also enabled other co-opted members from partner organisations to contribute towards debates and decisions on the delivery of local services. This in turn, as reported by the interviewees, has enabled fire services to operate in a way that involved the representatives of local communities in the service's decision-making process, thus making the service more accountable to communities. Senior managers found local councillors, as well as PCCs and other community representatives on FRAs, to be bringing an understanding of the needs of local people. This is because they have connections with their constituents, hold meetings and surgeries within their local areas and therefore they can bring up any issues raised by the communities into the FRA meetings.

The PFCC model of governance was introduced, inter alia, to improve accountability to the public. PFCCs have been portrayed as directly elected individuals who are meant to be directly engaging with their communities. FRSs that adopted the PFCC governance model found that their PFCC, despite being a politician elected to improve accountability to the public, had in fact less direct engagement with their constituents than the FRA members:

> *I don't know of any member of the public that's contacted the PFCC to hold us to account for anything. (CFO, Case Study 5)*

> *Obviously the PFCC hasn't got the time to go out, although [the PFCC] does go out and visit fire stations, has done, it's probably more of a challenge for a PFCC to have that sort of local impact that the [FRA] member potentially would have had previously. (Director of Finance, Case Study 5)*

Participants found the single-person governance to be difficult in terms of responsiveness to the residents and fire service needs. Some senior managers said that it was impractical or unfeasible in terms of capacity and capability on a day-to-day basis.

Although the level of public interest in fire services remained low, participants found that sufficient communications channels for residents were in place to directly contact their PFCC. For example, PFCCs held surgeries for their constituents. There was also an opportunity for local people to speak to the Office of the PFCC. Some interviewees believed that the PFCC model of governance provided more accountability because it offered more direct communication channels than the FRA governance model. However, there were also contrary views that the FRA was more accountable. FRA members represented their local areas and had day-to-day direct contact with their communities, whereas, although some PFCCs held surgeries with the public, they were not very well attended and PFCCs did not have sufficient resources to actively engage with the constituents at a local level.

Horizontal Accountability

In this subsection, horizontal political accountability relationships are discussed following the introduction of the Policing and Crime Act 2017. Horizontal accountability continued to be important between individuals operating and collaborating in the same areas of interest, which is the safety of their local communities. This primarily involved personal relationships between fire officers and politicians (FRA members or PFCCs) at the leadership level.

Personal Relationships Between Officers and Politicians

In the FRA governance model, the relationships between senior officers and local councillors remained crucial to working towards developing the right policies and strategies for their local service and for the best interest of the public. Since the 2017 legislation and PCCs being able to sit on FRAs, a closer relationship between senior officers and PCCs developed. Some senior officers were concerned that this might encourage PCCs to go ahead and develop a business case to take over the governance of their local FRS. They found having a good working relationship with their PCC as crucial in maintaining the existing governance arrangements. Maintaining healthy governance relationships between the senior officer and politicians, including PCCs, within the FRSs, was perceived as very important by managers, as it could obviate the desire of PCCs from taking over the governance of their local service.

Under the PFCC model of governance, the relationship between officers and politicians has also been important. The relationship between CFO and

PFCC, both ultimately responsible for their fire service, has become crucial to the success of the PFCC governance model. CFO and PFCC have on many occasions been accompanied by Chief Constable responsible for policing, as both police and FRS worked towards maintaining or improving community safety within their area.

> *The relationship is very important... the relationship between a PFCC and a CFO, or a chief constable, is one built upon trust, one built upon mutual respect, and one built upon the needs of the community... to ensure that we're not always going to agree but we've got to have that safe environment to be able to bounce ideas between all parties. (DCFO, Case Study 5)*

The relationship between PFCCs, CFOs and Chief Constables was built on informal mutual accountability during private discussions. The discussions were formal as well as informal, but all focussed upon the safety of local communities. In the early stages, they were crucial as the senior officers had to pass the knowledge and understanding about the fire service, including direction of travel and community needs and aspirations, to PFCCs to be able to allow them to fulfil their role in the most effective manner. However, on many occasions, the relationship between CFOs and PFCCs was challenged, mainly because of the political nature and objectives of PFCCs. Senior officers tried to persuade them to make decisions based upon operational matters and the safety of the public rather than political aspirations.

Overall, in both governance models, the relationship between officers and politicians was seen as a significant element of sound governance arrangements and ultimately the common service objective of keeping local people safe. However, the relationship appeared more of a personal matter in the PFCC governance model, where a collective dialogue between three individuals takes place to ensure that they hold each other accountable for safety of the public.

Diagonal Accountability

In this subsection, diagonal political accountability relationships are discussed following the introduction of the Policing and Crime Act 2017. Diagonal accountability relationships continued to play a significant role under political accountability. FRSs through their governing bodies have remained indirectly accountable to political parties and representative bodies.

Local and National Politics

Party-political affiliation remained an important factor in political accountability relationships. In all six areas examined in this study, there was a mixture of Labour, Conservative and Independent leadership in the FRAs, while all three of the PFCC-governed services were led by Conservatives.

Under the FRA governance arrangements, PCCs from the Conservative Party were more interested in taking over the governance of their local FRSs than PCCs from other political parties. In one case study, the fact that the PCC and the FRA were both Labour Party affiliated meant that they mostly agreed about the strategy for the service. In Case Study 1, the Labour PCC was open about not seeing a need to take over the FRS's governance. On the other hand, the Conservative PCC from Case Study 3 was interested in a potential transfer from a Conservative-led FRA to the PFCC model. This suggests that the same political party affiliation of the PCC, as well as the FRA or the county council, facilitates developing a complementary approach to FRSs. However, a more politically diverse FRA with opposing politicians might be more likely to effectively scrutinise the service and ask challenging questions.

Under the PFCC governance model, PFCCs can belong to a political party or can be independent, although most PCCs have an affiliation to a political party. All four PFCCs that have taken over the governance of their local FRSs have been associated with the Conservative Party. The PCCs were nominated by their political parties and then elected by their local communities. Interviewees also felt that Conservative PFCCs were closer to the central Conservative government than the FRA members.

> *I think PFCCs are much closer to the Home Office than FRA members... I know for a fact my PFCC on various issues has directly rung up the Home Office or spoken to the minister in person about things, whereas that's very, very rare for a FRA member to do that, even the chair of a FRA to have that type of direct relationship with central government. (CFO, Case Study 4)*

> *I think we are more accountable because of the PFCC and because of their political standing. (Director of Finance, Case Study 5)*

FRSs, through PFCCs, felt more accountable to central government than before under FRAs because of the PFCCs' political positions. The Conservative party ideology and its policies, which the PFCCs generally agreed with, have indirectly influenced the FRS's decisions. This could come directly from their local political party or the national political party, or from the Conservative central government, all complicating the accountability relationships of the PFCC, but clearly influencing their relationship with the CFO and senior managers. This suggests that the PFCCs, when scrutinising their local FRSs, have been influenced by party-political affiliations. PFCCs felt accountable, at least to some degree, to party leaders for their positions, as they had been nominated by their political parties. They were chosen from a list of candidates for the PFCC position by the party members. As a result, PFCCs generally aligned themselves with party-political positions. Firefighters also found PFCCs to be heavily influenced by their party politics as well as the political agenda from central government. Most found the governance transfer to be a political manoeuvre to gain political power over their local FRS. PFCCs felt largely accountable to their political parties and have been able to introduce and implement their party-political (Conservative) ambitions into FRSs. National and local political parties have had no powers to enforce PFCCs' compliance with party-political agenda. However, the consequences for PFCCs might nevertheless be significant if they are expelled from, or disciplined by, their political party.

Representative Bodies

Political accountability between the representative bodies and the FRS has remained important after the introduction of the Policing and Crime Act 2017. In FRA-governed services, the representative bodies continued to have a strong political influence on the service. The unions have had a significant influence over the FRSs. For example, in one service, the local FBU branch was promoting the transfer of governance to a PFCC model as opposed to remaining under the FRA, while in others, it favoured the FRA model.

Under the PFCC governance model, the FBU continued to represent firefighters, and in some cases, challenged PFCCs' decisions. For example, pressures from the FBU caught one PFCC off guard and were seen as having created adverse publicity for the FRS. This has had an effect on the political standing of the PFCCs and ultimately affected the PFCC's chances of getting re-elected in the elections. However, in some cases, the participants also found that the FBU had a remarkably good relationship with PFCCs, which was based on mutual respect and an open-door policy to discuss fire matters.

Overall, the representative bodies, most notably the FBU, continued to have a strong political influence on the service following the implementation of the Policing and Crime Act 2017. They have been representing firefighters and challenging advice and/or decisions put forward by the service, the governing bodies or the government. FRAs and PFCCs have been consequently mindful of the representative bodies' demands.

Conclusion

This chapter discussed FRSs' understandings of political accountability before and after the introduction of the Policing and Crime Act 2017. Table 4 summarises FRSs' understandings of political accountability in relation to vertical, horizontal and diagonal directions.

Before the Policing and Crime Act 2017, the public were theoretically able to hold their local FRAs to account indirectly. The FRA governance model has enabled local councillors, who sit on FRAs, to be directly elected by voters, although not directly elected to sit on FRAs. In practice, under the FRA governance model, residents had limited powers to hold FRA members to account and/or dismiss them. After the introduction of the 2017 legislation, in services that remained under the FRA governance model, the residents continued to indirectly choose their FRA members. However, the 2017 Act enabled a directly elected PCC (or a PCC representative) to join the FRA. Since 2017, in services that have adopted the PFCC governance model, residents are able to directly elect an individual politician in local PCC/PFCC elections. The public are also able to dismiss their PFCC, if they are not pleased with the politician, by electing another individual in local elections.

Before and after the introduction of the Policing and Crime Act 2017, political decision-making played an important role under both governance models. However, both senior managers and front-line staff felt that the PFCC governance model resulted in more politicisation because of one politician accountable for the service, whereas under the FRA governance model, there were several people involved who could step in and debate decisions. Notwithstanding the increase in political decision-making, senior officers found post-2017 FRAs and PFCCs to be more politically accountable to local people than pre-2017 FRAs, as they were more representative of their communities when making final decisions, for which they were accountable.

Public engagement in both governance models has been relatively low, both before and after the Policing and Crime Act 2017. Residents have not been involved in the decision-making of their local FRS, although they have had a number of opportunities to be engaged in services' planning. Following the introduction of the 2017 legislation, FRA members continued to represent

Table 4. FRSs' Understandings on Political Accountability Before and After the Introduction of the Policing and Crime Act 2017.

		Before the 2017 Act	After the 2017 Act	
Directions	**Main Sub-Themes**	**FRA-Governed Services**	**FRA-Governed Services**	**PFCC-Governed Services**
Vertical (governing body – communities)	Local elections and representation	*Limited* ability to dismiss FRA members	*Moderate* ability to dismiss FRA members, including the PCC	*Extensive* ability to directly dismiss the PFCC
	Decision-making	*Moderate* accountability in terms of political agenda on FRA	*Moderate* accountability in terms of political agenda on FRA.	*Limited* accountability in terms of political agenda on FRA.
	Public engagement and transparency	*Limited* opportunities for the public to engage with the service *Moderate* transparency	*Limited* opportunities for the public to engage with the service *Moderate* transparency	*Extensive* opportunities for the public to engage with the service *Limited* transparency
	Responsiveness to communities	*Moderate* level of connections with local areas and communities	*Moderate* level of connections with local areas and communities	*Limited* level of connections with local areas and communities
Horizontal (senior managers – governing body)	Personal relationships	*Moderate* level of mutual accountability working towards policies and strategies	*Moderate* level of mutual accountability working towards policies and strategies	*Extensive* level of mutual accountability working towards policies and strategies
Diagonal (FRS – political party/ representative body)	Local and national politics	*Moderate* level of influence of political parties on FRAs' decision-making	*Moderate* level of influence of political parties on FRAs' decision-making	*Extensive* level of influence of political parties on PFCCs' decision-making
	Representative bodies	*Moderate* level of influence of representative bodies on FRAs' decision-making	*Moderate* level of influence of representative bodies on FRAs' decision-making	*Extensive* level of influence of representative bodies on PFCCs' decision-making

Source: Author's interpretation.

their local areas and had day-to-day direct contact with their constituents. In contrast, although PFCCs held various engagements with local public, they were not very well attended and PFCCs did not have sufficient resources to directly engage with constituents at a local level. The PFCC governance model introduced greater opportunities for communities to actively take part in the services' decision-making processes, but it also brought limited transparency arrangements, which ultimately reduced possibilities to actively hold PFCCs to account.

FRSs and FRAs/PFCCs also held each other horizontally to account when working collaboratively in the interest of local communities. In both governance models, a good working relationship between senior officers and politicians was perceived as a sign of sound governance arrangements and ultimately the common service objective of keeping the local public safe. The relationship appeared more of a constructive debate in the PFCC governance model between PFCCs, CFOs and Chief Constables. Nonetheless, a closer relationship between PCCs and senior officers as well as local councillors also developed under the reformed FRA model.

FRSs have also been diagonally accountable to political parties and various representative bodies. Under this type of accountability, there are no powers to enforce compliance; however, the consequences from political parties and representative bodies could still be significant. FRAs and PFCCs tended to vote party-politically and ultimately were taking decisions in line with their party's political policy or strategy, whereas trade unions were often pressuring the services to change their policies.

Overall, FRSs felt that the Policing and Crime Act 2017 brought greater focus on political accountability in all three directions. However, political or individual priorities continued to be a distortion of FRSs' accountability in both governance models.

REFERENCES

Department for Communities and Local Government (DCLG). (2012). *Fire and rescue national framework for England*. DCLG.

Department for Communities and Local Government (DCLG). (2015). *Local government transparency code 2015*. DCLG.

Home Office. (2018). *Fire and rescue national framework for England*. Home Office.

Mulgan, R. (2003). *Holding power to account: Accountability in modern democracies*. Palgrave Macmillan.

Romzek, B. S., & Dubnick, M. J. (1987). Accountability in the public sector: Lessons from the Challenger tragedy. *Public Administration Review*, 47(3), 227–238.

5

FINDINGS: LEGAL ACCOUNTABILITY

ABSTRACT

This chapter examines the dynamics of legal accountability within English Fire and Rescue Services (FRSs) before and after the governance reforms introduced by the Policing and Crime Act 2017. Using Romzek and Dubnick's (1987) framework, it explores vertical, horizontal and diagonal accountability relationships and their changes under two governance models: Fire and Rescue Authorities (FRAs) and Police, Fire and Crime Commissioners (PFCCs). Prior to 2017, legal accountability was primarily associated with the vertical dimension of accountability, enshrined in the statutory requirements such as the Fire and Rescue Services Act 2004 and Civil Contingencies Act 2004 and reinforced through financial compliance and audit mechanisms. However, the abolition of the Audit Commission and subsequent austerity localism weakened external scrutiny. The 2017 reforms introduced PFCC governance model with new reporting obligations and a legal duty to collaborate with other emergency services while reinstating external inspections through His Majesty's Inspectorate of Constabulary and Fire & Rescue Services (HMICFRS). These changes strengthened diagonal accountability and formalised partnerships, particularly with police forces. Despite improvements, concerns remain about the inspectorate's independence and fragmented governance structures caused by diverse funding arrangements. This chapter concludes that reforms enhanced legal accountability but did not fully resolve tensions between FRSs' autonomy, central oversight and political influence.

Keywords: Legal accountability; fire and rescue services; governance reform; public administration; directions of accountability

INTRODUCTION

Following the analysis of political accountability relationships in Chapter 4, this chapter focuses on the dynamics of legal accountability in English Fire and Rescue Services (FRSs), where perceptions of accountability change as result of governance reforms introduced by the Policing and Crime Act 2017. Legal accountability is similar to bureaucratic accountability (Chapter 3), in which it involves the frequent application of control to a wide range of activities. However, in contrast to bureaucratic accountability, the source of control in legal accountability is external rather than internal to the organisation (Romzek & Dubnick, 1987).

FRSs are in a legal accountability relationship with a number of external stakeholders who can impose legal sanctions and assert obligations if FRSs violate the law. They primarily include central government departments but also the courts or other government bodies, particularly when incidents result in fatalities. Legal accountability can be mandatory or discretionary. When legal accountability is mandated, this means that it applies to all FRSs. If it is discretionary, FRSs have the right to undertake the role or action but are under no obligation to do so.

This chapter describes FRSs' understandings of legal accountability in relation to the vertical, horizontal and diagonal directions of accountability, which address the '*accountability for what*' and '*accountability to whom*' dimensions of the conceptual framework, introduced in Chapter 2. More specifically, this chapter examines how these understandings have changed in the context of the governance reforms brought in by the Policing and Crime Act 2017 (see Figs. 7 and 8).

ACCOUNTABILITY ARRANGEMENTS PRIOR TO THE POLICING AND CRIME ACT 2017

Vertical Accountability

Legal accountability is primarily interpreted with regard to the vertical direction of accountability with direct hierarchical lines of command between FRSs and other stakeholders. In this section, the sub-themes of statutory requirements, financial compliance and audit arrangements are discussed within the vertical dimension of legal accountability prior to the introduction of the Policing and Crime Act 2017.

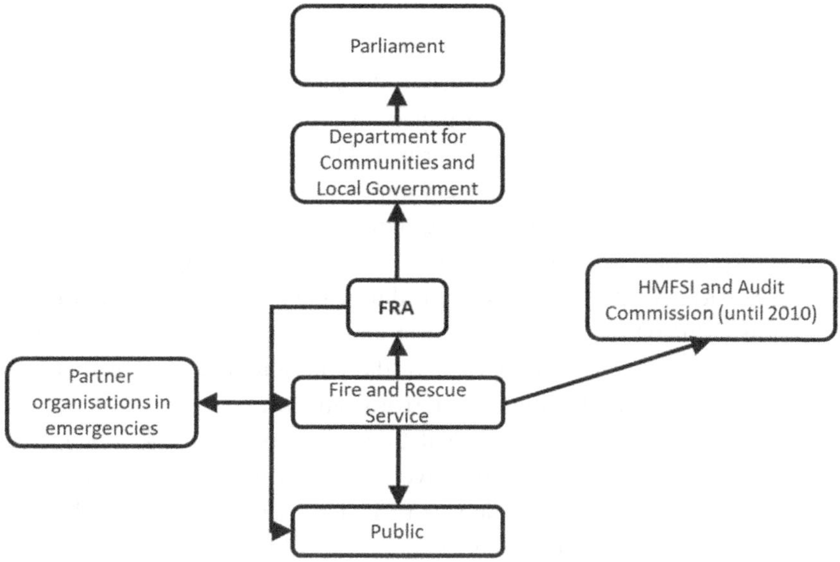

Source: Author's interpretation.

Fig. 7. Fire and Rescue Services' Understandings of Legal Accountability Relationships in FRA-Governed Fire and Rescue Services Before the Introduction of the Policing and Crime Act 2017.

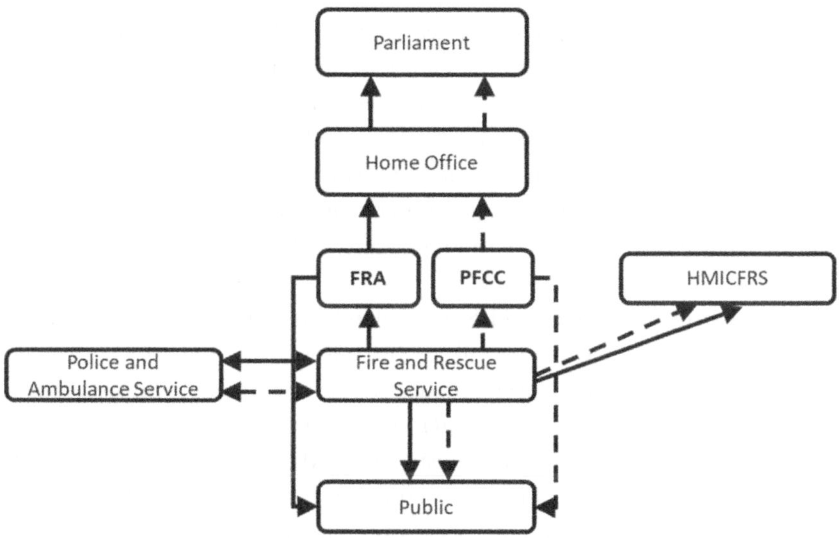

Source: Author's interpretation.

Fig. 8. Fire and Rescue Services' Understandings of Legal Accountability Relationships in FRA-Governed (Solid Lines) and in PFCC-Governed (Dotted Lines) Fire and Rescue Services After the Introduction of the Policing and Crime Act 2017.

Statutory Requirements

FRSs' legal accountability is enshrined in the statutory requirements through both primary legislation (see Murphy et al., 2020, p. 19) and secondary legislation. Primary legislation is the principal legislation that has been passed by Parliament whereas secondary legislation interprets and provides guidance on the implementation of primary legislation. The most significant piece of primary legislation that FRSs have been required to follow is the Fire and Rescue Services Act 2004. It clarifies the duties and powers of Fire and Rescue Authorities (FRAs) to fight fires, protect and prevent people and properties from fires, rescue people from road traffic collisions and deal with other emergencies, including flooding and terrorist attacks.

Alongside this legislation, the Civil Contingencies Act 2004 outlines the roles, responsibilities and collaborative arrangements that FRSs (amongst others) must put in place in response to major civil emergencies. FRSs are identified as Category 1 responders under the Civil Contingencies Act 2004, together with police, ambulance services, local authorities, the Environment Agency and NHS bodies (Murphy & Lakoma, 2023). Their role is to plan for, prevent and respond to emergencies at the local level and to collaborate with Category 1 and 2 responders at larger and more complex civil emergencies, whether at local, regional or national levels. FRSs have been vertically accountable under the Civil Contingencies Act 2004 to whoever is the lead agency when in an emergency. The lead agency (whether it is police, fire or ambulance service) is based on the nature of an incident.

FRSs have also been required to follow secondary legislation, most notably the national framework, first introduced in 2004. This operationalised the Fire and Rescue Services Act 2004 and imposed detailed objectives, priorities and requirements on the services. Subsequent National Frameworks have been introduced over the years to update and replace the priorities for FRSs (see Table 5).

The department overseeing FRSs in England has a duty to produce a policy and operational framework for all English FRSs. The Home Office passed responsibility for the fire service to the Department for Transport, Local Government and the Regions (DTLR) in 2001, which then transferred it to the Office of the Deputy Prime Minister (ODPM) in 2003, and the Department of Communities and Local Government (DCLG) in 2005 (Raynsford, 2016), before being transferred back to the Home Office in January 2016. Senior managers had mixed feelings about these changes at the national level and the ultimate transfer of responsibilities back to the Home Office.

Table 5. Fire and Rescue Services' National Frameworks Prior to 2017.

Version	Title	Content	Department	Publication Date	Period
1	The FRS National Framework 2004/2005	The duty of best value and the importance of achieving continuous improvement Integrated risk management plans (IRMPs)	ODPM	July 2004	1 year
2	The Fire and Rescue National Framework 2005/2006	Partnership working with FRAs Comprehensive performance assessment	ODPM	December 2004	1 year
3	The Fire and Rescue National Framework 2006–2008	Greater emphasis on the delivery of equality and diversity	ODPM	April 2006	2 years
4	FRS National Framework 2008–11	Delivery of an enhanced resilience capability Identification of new threats and challenges	DCLG	May 2008	3 years
5	Fire and Rescue National Framework for England	Strengthened 'downwards' accountability between fire and rescue authorities (FRAs) and local communities Shifted primary responsibility from the government to the FRAs	DCLG	July 2012	Open ended

Source: Author and adapted from ODPM (2004a), ODPM (2004b), ODPM (2006), DCLG (2008), DCLG (2012).

I think... the fire service can experience a little bit of benign neglect coming under the Home Office, because the Home Office is very much around the policing and security agenda, with fire being such a small part of that. (Director of Response, Case Study 4)

The move to the Home Office was not welcomed by FRSs because of its long-term relationship with police services and the introduction of similar requirements and similar performance metrics for FRSs as for the police.

Notwithstanding their views on the transfer, FRSs felt accountable to the Home Office, as the government department overseeing the fire sector. FRSs have been required to regularly report to the Home Office. For example, they have been required to submit data and publish statutory documents in accordance with the National Framework, including an annual statement of assurance of compliance, an Integrated Risk Management Plan (IRMP) and their financial plans. All three latter documents provided assurance to the government on financial, governance and operational matters.

FRSs' compliance with the requirements enshrined in the National Framework is reviewed bi-annually by the Secretary of State in a report to Parliament under Section 25 of the Fire and Rescue Services Act 2004. This involved checking if all FRA-governed services published the three statutory documents and reviewing general compliance with the National Framework. If an FRS did not comply with the National Framework, the Secretary of State was required to state any steps taken to achieve compliance. The Secretaries of State have been providing the bi-annual reports to Parliament, but in the 13 years before the introduction of the Policing and Crime Act 2017, they did not use the legislative power of non-compliance (Murphy & Lakoma, 2020).

To comply with the legislative requirements, services have been delegating some legal accountability to individuals, called statutory officers. Statutory officers are accountable for undertaking their legal roles and responsibilities. However, central government has the power to enforce compliance only on the services rather than individuals. All standalone FRA-governed services (combined and metropolitan services) have been required to have three statutory officers:

(1) Chief Executive (known as the Head of Paid Service or Chief Fire Officer [CFO]);

(2) Section 151 Officer (usually the Chief Financial Officer or Director of Finance);

(3) Monitoring Officer (usually the Head of Legal Services or Legal Advisor).

In county council FRA-governed services, the county council is responsible for appointing these positions. The CFO's role is to manage the FRSs' staff, services and equipment for the purpose of delivery of the statutory functions enshrined in the FRSs' legislation (Local Government and Housing Act 1989). The Section 151 Officer is responsible for maintaining the financial integrity of the FRA (Local Government Act 1972) while the Monitoring Officer's role is to ensure that the FRA acts within and through the law (Local Government and Housing Act 1989). County council FRAs are integral part of county councils, which means that FRSs are ultimately accountable to the county council's Chief Executive, Section 151 Officer and Monitoring Officer. In practice, county council FRA services had less control over their services as they did not have their own Chief Executive, Section 151 Officer or Monitoring Officer responsible for legally holding the services to account. In some cases, they had not been adequately held to account for the use of their budgets, ultimately resulting in financial problems within their services (Case Study 3 and Case Study 4).

FRSs have also been scrutinised by Parliament, by two select committees of the House of Commons. The first was the Communities and Local Government Committee until 2015, but became the Home Affairs Committee after the transfer of fire responsibilities to the Home Office in 2016, and the second was the Public Accounts Committee (PAC, 2016). These committees of MPs have had the right to call ministers, officials and other individuals to give written or oral evidence. Select committees scrutinise the work of government departments and investigate specific issues. They call for evidence, ask questions, publish reports and demand responses from ministers and departments. Select committees are seen as mechanisms for ensuring transparency and accountability in government.

Overall, the department in charge of FRSs' policy legally holds the services to account for compliance with the legislation. It represents a legal accountability relationship between two autonomous parties, where the government (and ultimately Parliament) controls the services and has the right to impose legal sanctions upon them. Legal accountability requirements also cascade down to those individuals within FRSs responsible for statutory roles although central government has the power to enforce compliance only on the services rather than on individuals.

Financial Compliance

Financial compliance implies legally holding a service accountable for their financial activities. FRSs, represented by FRA members, have a fiduciary duty to the council's taxpayers. This meant that FRAs have been required to set a lawful annual budget, matching its income with its outgoings.

Central government was traditionally the primary source of funding for FRSs in the form of central government grants (called 'revenue support grants' and 'top-up' funds). However, central government financial support has continuously reduced since 2010 as result of austerity localism (Lowndes & Pratchett, 2012). This meant that FRAs had to mitigate the impact of continually reduced funding from central government and have sought to raise more funding through local council taxes via a precept, which is a portion of council tax allocated to the FRS, and/or business rates.

> *We're responsible to the taxpayer, both nationally and locally, so locally through the collection of business rates and council tax and then also nationally through the receipt of the government grants and the top-up money that we receive from national government where we're obviously accountable to the wider taxpayer as well, right through to the police and fire minister. (Director 1, Case Study 1)*

Senior managers felt legally accountable for how they were spending their funding at both national and local levels, upwards to the central government and downwards to the public. The department overseeing FRSs at the time (DCLG) was responsible for distributing annual funding on behalf of Her Majesty's Treasury via an annual local government finance settlement to all FRAs. Combined FRAs and metropolitan FRAs have been receiving their funding directly from central government whereas county council FRAs have had their funding allocated by their county council. As separate entities having their standalone budget, combined FRAs (Case Study 1, 5, and 6) and metropolitan FRAs (Case Study 2) were able to set and raise their own council tax precept. In contrast, county council FRAs could not raise their own precept, as their budgets were included within the county council's precept (Case Study 3 and 4). This meant that county council FRAs on occasion had to negotiate and align their budgets to other departments within the county council. This ultimately affected their accountability down to local communities receiving the services. FRSs governed by county council FRAs felt less accountable to central government and local communities because they could not raise their own precept and ultimately had no direct say on what percentage of the overall precept they receive, the opposite was true for standalone FRSs, as they were in control of setting and raising their own precept (subject to council tax capping arrangements).

Audit

Legal requirements, in the form of external as well as internal audit, act as mechanisms that underpin accountability. Both forms of audit enable service providers to be held accountable to stakeholders, the government and the public. Internal audit in local government has been subject to the Accounts and Audit Regulations 2015, following the Local Accountability and Audit 2014 Act, and involved assessing governance, risk management and internal control systems. The focus on external audit has been twofold: first, it involved an independent opinion about the service's financial health on an annual basis and second, it examined both efficiency and effectiveness in the use of resources.

Before the Local Accountability and Audit 2014 Act, the Audit Commission undertook Comprehensive Performance Assessments (CPAs) for all FRSs in England between 2005 and 2008, which were followed by Comprehensive Area Assessments (CAAs) in 2009. The Commission assessed FRSs' strategic and operational performance with an annual direction of travel assessment and a use of resources judgement and published an overall service assessment of the services (Murphy & Greenhalgh, 2018). The assessments were also accompanied by the possibility of government intervention. Government intervention became a possibility when service standards fell below minimum requirements (Martin, 2000). Section 22 of the Fire and Rescue Services Act 2004 states that the department responsible for FRSs should intervene, on behalf of the public, if an FRA fails, or is likely to fail, to deliver its duty of Best Value (the requirement to facilitate 'continuous improvement') or to act in accordance with the National Framework. Between 2005 and 2007, the Audit Commission identified eight FRAs as requiring improvement and support in accordance with the framework (Coleman, 2009). Accordingly, the department overseeing FRSs established an 'engagement' process with each of the eight FRAs, which proved to be successful as all FRAs improved their performance (Coleman, 2009).

In 2010, the closure of the Audit Commission and termination of CAAs were announced. Alongside the Audit Commission's demise, the Local Audit and Accountability Act 2014 introduced a new auditing regime, supposedly to achieve greater local accountability. It moved away from reporting to central government and introduced more fragmented arrangements under the policy of austerity localism (Lowndes & Pratchett, 2012). Henceforth, the National Audit Office (NAO) had to provide central government with reports into value for money and financial sustainability in FRSs. Operational performance management became the legal responsibility of local FRAs. FRAs' legal reporting requirements reduced, and reporting focused on services' financial conformance rather than operational performance (Ferry & Eckersley, 2015). In addition, the NAO also took over the oversight role for the local public audit of FRAs. External auditors undertook audits and were able to issue Public Interest Reports, as part of the value for money reporting, which informed the public and the Secretary of State about any significant financial matters (Murphy & Lakoma, 2021).

Senior managers were acutely aware that FRSs had had a series of different types of auditing regimes and scrutiny arrangements at a national level through different governments throughout the last 20 years. However, this constant churn and uncertainty increased their concerns about the effectiveness of these arrangements. Changes in government policies for FRSs contributed to inconsistent and very limited scrutiny arrangements during these years. Some of those interviewed even believed that after the closure of the Audit Commission and before the introduction of the 2017 legislation, there was a lack of FRSs' legal accountability to central government.

> *When we started with austerity, government removed all interest in stats and outcomes from fire services, we were kind of cast adrift. (CFO, Case Study 1)*

> *The push to localism...at some points has enabled fire services to really do what they wanted, with virtually no accountability to anybody I think. (Director 1, Case Study 1)*

> *I couldn't understand localism...we all do the same thing, we have the same set up, we have the same legislation but there were so many different ways of doing it. (Area Manager 2, Case Study 3)*

Although central government remained accountable for FRSs' financial conformance, most senior managers believed that the fire sector had suffered 'neglect' from central government. This is because the scrutiny regime on operational performance was removed, which consequently weakened legal accountability towards central government as result of the policy of austerity localism. As a result, FRSs had to determine their local standards, response times and other performance indicators and become professionally accountable under the sector-led improvement regime.

Horizontal Accountability

In this subsection, legal accountability in the horizontal direction is discussed. It primarily involves organisations that are equal to one another working together as result of the existing legislation in place. Typically, more negotiation and collaboration than vertical command takes place under this direction of accountability.

Legal Partnerships

Before the introduction of the Policing and Crime Act 2017, there was no mandatory legal duty imposed on FRSs to collaborate with other emergency services. Although engagements and partnership working had been enabled and encouraged by the Local Government Acts 1999; 2000, the Civil Contingencies Act 2004 and the Crime and Disorder Act 1998, FRSs were not legally mandated to collaboratively respond to them with other partners, other than in a major civil emergency.

The Crime and Disorder Act 1998 created local Crime and Disorder Partnerships and made FRSs designated public bodies, multiply and severally responsible for reducing or mitigating crime and disorder (including anti-social behaviour) in their local communities. FRSs along with police and other local authorities were involved in implementing strategies for the reduction of crime and disorder in their local areas. Although FRSs did not indicate whether that partnership was an accountability relationship, they nonetheless shared the same objectives of community safety with other organisations and continued to assist each other with their day-to-day work.

Second, Local Strategic Partnerships (LSPs), established by the Local Government Acts 1999 and 2000, provided the legal framework for additional horizontal accountability relationships and vehicles for negotiating Local Area Agreements (LAAs). LAAs were agreements between central government and local areas designed to improve locally delivered public services. FRSs, along with other organisations from the local statutory, voluntary, community and private sectors, addressed local problems and discussed local strategies and initiatives. LAAs generally aimed to encourage joint working and community involvement at the local level, until they too were abolished in 2010.

The third horizontal accountability relationship, in which FRSs have been involved, is based on the provisions of the Civil Contingencies Act 2004, which addressed major civil contingencies and emergencies. The 2004 legislation established local, regional and national risk registrars, resilience forums and collaborative responsibilities on designated Category 1 and Category 2 responder organisations, with FRSs being a designated Category 1 responder. FRSs have been active members of Local Resilience Forums with other local organisations, which aim to plan and prepare for major incidents and catastrophic emergencies. As a result of the Civil Contingencies Act 2004, FRSs have been legally obliged to respond to emergencies with other local partners.

Diagonal Accountability

Legal requirements that manifest themselves in the form of diagonal accountability include, most significantly, independent inspectorates and external auditing bodies. These are not part of the direct central government controls, but their roles and functions are established by statute, and they independently publish reports to government, Parliament and the public on services' performance and the meeting of standards. This means that they do not hold the services directly to account; however, they have a significant influence on both individual services and the sector collectively because of who they report to. Inspectorates and external auditing bodies also ultimately provide the relevant information that enables parliamentarians to hold services to account.

Independent Inspectorate

The origins of the first inspectorate for English fire services, Her/His Majesty's Fire Service Inspectorate (HMFSI), dates back to 1947 (OPSR, 2003; Ewen, 2009). The fire inspectorate, however, did not hold fire services to account. Its role was primarily to provide the sector with advice on compliance with fire standards. Senior managers felt that HMFSI had become outdated and ineffective in providing an accurate assessment of FRAs towards the end of its existence. They perceived it as a weak source of accountability, as it resembled a body that was established to provide the sector with standards rather than directly hold services to account.

In 2005, the Audit Commission took on the role of external inspection and brought FRSs under their national assessment regimes. HMFSI was closed in 2007. After the announcement of the abolition of the Audit Commission, England remained without an independent inspectorate for the fire service for next eight years (Murphy et al., 2020). At that time, FRSs did not feel accountable for their performance.

> *We'd previously been audited by the Audit Commission, so there's been various level of scrutiny about performance of fire services over previous years, but when we got into the period of austerity, government removed quango departments such as Audit Commission and HMFSI, and I guess you've had a perfect storm is a way I'd describe it.... Nobody was looking at efficiency and effectiveness, nobody was holding us to account for that really. (DCFO, Case Study 3)*

Following the termination of external inspections, FRSs were subjected to sector-led peer assessments (see Chapter 6). They were supposed to improve accountability at a local level, but the results were neither robust nor transparent.

> *So, I was fairly horrified back in 2010 when the Audit Commission was to be ... removed...it was replaced with peer review... and they served a purpose, but they were a little bit too cosy, and I missed the independence of an external inspectorate. (CFO, Case Study 6)*

Overall, legal accountability in the diagonal direction was very limited and the government resolved to change it. The next section of this chapter moves on to explain understandings of legal accountability following the implementation of the Policing and Crime Act 2017.

ACCOUNTABILITY ARRANGEMENTS AFTER THE POLICING AND CRIME ACT 2017

Vertical Accountability

This subsection discusses understandings of legal vertical accountability in the FRA governance model ('the representation model') and the Police, Fire and Crime Commissioner (PFCC) model ('the governance model') following the implementation of the Policing and Crime Act 2017.

Statutory Requirements

FRSs' legal accountability arrangements have remained enshrined in both primary and secondary legislation. Most of the legal provisions remained in place; however, some governance requirements included in the Fire and Rescue Services Act 2004 have been replaced as result of the Policing and Crime Act 2017. The Policing and Crime Act 2017 included significant provisions affecting both police and FRSs (see Chapter 1).

The 2012 National Framework also needed to be replaced to include the provisions enshrined in the 2017 legislation (Murphy et al., 2020). The National Framework was updated in 2018 (Home Office, 2018) and continued to provide national policy for all FRSs, albeit continuing with the policy of local governance and local accountability focused on the FRA/PFCC level. This meant that central government continued to play only a limited role in overseeing the fire and rescue sector. Both FRA- and PFCC-governed services have generally remained relatively free to run their services in a way that they considered to be the most efficient and effective (although they are still subject to the duty of Best Value). Although there was an increasing trend of moving away from national level accountability, the Home Secretary's report on FRSs', compliance with National Framework, and the intervention protocol for FRSs have all remained in place. This meant that the government has retained the power to intervene in services that are failing or likely to fail to meet their duty of Best Value.

The Home Office continued to be the primary department in charge of FRSs until April 2025. As such, the Home Office, and by extension FRSs, essentially continued to fall under the scrutiny of two select committees of the House of Commons: The Home Affairs Committee and the Public Accounts Committee. In April 2025, following the 2024 UK general election, the new Labour government confirmed a change that moved ministerial responsibility for all fire policy and functions from the Home Office to the Ministry of Housing, Communities and Local Government (MHCLG).

In FRA-governed services, public reporting requirements have remained the same as before the introduction of the Policing and Crime Act 2017. However, FRSs that transferred to the PFCC governance model have had their reporting requirements changed (Home Office, 2018). In addition to the statutory documents published by FRAs, a PFCC has to produce a Fire and Rescue Plan (or a joint Police, Crime and Fire and Rescue Plan) to set out the strategic vision, priorities and objectives for FRSs (if joint, for both fire and rescue and police service) and a Fire and Rescue Statement, which replaced the Annual Statement of Assurance. In addition, an internal body, called a

Police, Fire and Crime Panel scrutinises the Fire and Rescue Plan (or the joint Police, Crime and Fire and Rescue Plan). FRSs that experienced a transfer of governance to a PFCC also have to comply with different transparency requirements. Section 11 of the Police Reform and Social Responsibility Act 2011 and the Elected Local Policing Bodies (Specified Information) Order 2011 imposed equivalent provisions to those in the Local Government Acts, which include publishing senior officers' salaries, organisational charts, budgets, expenditures and records of decisions taken.

As with FRA-governed services, PFCCs are required to delegate legal accountability to statutory officers. The requirements for statutory officers are slightly different than in FRA-governed services. Police Reform and Social Responsibility Act 2011 states that PFCCs are required to appoint:

- a Chief Executive/Head of Paid Service, who is also designated as the Monitoring Officer;
- a Section 151 Officer.

The Chief Executive of the PFCC's office holds the role of the Monitoring Officer (Local Government and Housing Act 1989), supports the PFCC and assists in the delivery of all statutory duties. As with the FRA arrangements, the Section 151 Officer acts as a Chief Finance Officer (Local Government 1972 Act) and advises the PFCC on financial matters.

The PFCC, as a governing body of the FRS, has inherited legal accountability for the service from the former FRA. Interestingly, some PFCCs, according to senior managers, did not explicitly understand what legal accountabilities they had inherited when it came to the transfer of responsibilities under their control.

> *I don't think before the change the PFCC fully understood the level of responsibility that he had inherited...what the PFCC can't divest is the accountability under that legislation... And I think it was a bit of a shock at the first meeting when we passed the PFCC all that legislation and said, there you go, this is what you've inherited! (DCFO, Case Study 5)*

PFCCs are legally responsible and if anything goes wrong, for example, a firefighter dies, they are the individuals that would be held to account, according to the Corporate Manslaughter and Homicide Act 2007. They are also legally accountable as the FRSs' employer under the following acts: Health and Safety at Work Act 1974, the Civil Contingencies Act 2004, the

Equalities Act 2010 and The Management of Health and Safety at Work Regulations 1999.

Financial Compliance

FRSs have remained accountable to a number of stakeholders for how they manage their funding. Besides publishing financial statements, they have been legally obliged to produce a medium-term financial plan, an efficiency plan and a reserves strategy as result of the 2018 National Framework (Home Office, 2018). Combined FRAs, metropolitan FRAs and PFCC-governed services need to publish these documents themselves as standalone organisations whereas county council FRAs are required to publish them within the county council's documentation.

Funding has continued to largely originate from council taxes, business rates and central government grants, making FRSs accountable to their communities as well as the government. Central government funding has continued to be delivered through the annual local government finance settlement in the form of revenue support grant and business rate retention. Combined FRAs, metropolitan FRAs and PFCC-governed services have been receiving their funding directly from central government whereas county council FRAs have had their funding allocated by their county council.

As separate entities having standalone budgets, combined FRAs, metropolitan FRAs and PFCC-governed services have been able to set and raise their own council tax precept. County council FRAs have continued to be included within the county council's precept. In addition, in PFCC-governed services, PFCCs have been required to establish a fire fund to ensure that there are two separate budgets for fire and police.

> *My concern is...there are different governance arrangements, services operate in different ways, in terms of their income and how their budgets are set, some authorities' budget is set more so via council tax, others ... and business rates, others is more set by a central government grant, it ... and there's so many variations, I think it dilutes governance to some extent. So, I ... personally, I'm a strong believer that they need to set some common governance arrangements. (Area Manager 2, Case Study 4)*

Senior managers acknowledged that each governance model received a different proportion of funding streams, which they felt was unsatisfactory. This was particularly the case in county council FRAs, where funding was often suspected of being 'lost' and/or subsidising other council services within the overall county council funding streams. These diverse funding arrangements have had therefore significant implications for accountability: standalone FRAs and PFCC-governed services have been directly accountable for financial compliance to the government and local communities whereas county council FRAs have been only indirectly accountable to these actors because their first relationship is with the county council.

Audit

Legal requirements in the form of external and internal audit have continued to act as mechanisms that underpinned accountability and assurance in the fire sector following the introduction of the Policing and Crime Act 2017. Audit provides an essential part of all accountability arrangements, as it certifies financial propriety. Internal audit in FRSs has remained concerned with assessing governance, risk management and internal control systems. The focus of external audit has remained predominantly financial and short-term (Murphy et al., 2023).

> *We've got internal audit that focuses very much on the governance within the service, how we do our business, and then you've got the external audit of things like the finances and the budgeting, all that kind of stuff. So, exponentially it's got massive effectively as a standalone organisation. (CFO, Case Study 4)*

Participants highlighted that standalone FRA-governed services and PFCC-governed services experienced greater auditing requirements than those services that were part of the county council's arrangements. This was because they have been required to be internally and externally audited as standalone organisations whereas county council FRAs' audits have been included in the county council auditing arrangements.

FRSs' financial conformance continued to be assessed by the NAO and then reported to central government. Operational performance management has not been directly assessed by the central government; however, it has been delegated to the new Her/His Majesty's Inspectorate of Constabulary and Fire & Rescue Services (HMICFRS).

Horizontal Accountability

This subsection deals with horizontal legal accountability relationships and concerns legal partnerships as result of the Policing and Crime Act 2017 that requires FRSs to work with other partners.

Legal Partnerships

FRSs, as result of the Policing and Crime Act 2017, have been legally required to collaborate with other emergency services, if it is in the interests of their efficiency or effectiveness. Although many interviewees argued that they had already been collaborating (particularly with the police), they stressed that the 2017 Act has meant that they need to demonstrate this more clearly.

> *We need to be absolutely clear on some of the legal elements, i.e., collaboration, we do absolutely need to ensure, whereas before it was the right thing to do or a good thing to do, we absolutely need to ensure we can demonstrate our attempts or our actual achievements with collaboration. (Finance Director, Case Study 2)*

> *We test and exercise with all our [Local] Resilience [Forum] partners, so that's local authorities, health, all the blue light services as well. So certainly, for me the Act hasn't changed anything in terms of how we collaborate. I think it's just put a focus on the sector and reminded some of those services that maybe haven't collaborated that well in the past that they absolutely should be, and they need to. (DCFO, Case Study 2)*

Alongside other local organisations, FRSs have remained active members of Local Resilience Forums. Interviewees pointed out that the 2017 legislation has strengthened and formalised collaboration between emergency services and partner organisations when preparing for local emergencies. It has particularly stressed the need for collaboration for those services that had not collaborated with other organisations before. This was tragically demonstrated in the response to the Grenfell Fire and the Manchester Arena attack, when local emergency services partially failed to respond to the emergencies and ultimately held each other to account for their response. The pandemic was also a catalyst for collaboration as FRSs helped ambulance services by driving vehicles, delivering medications, constructing vaccine stations and administering vaccines (Murphy & Lakoma, 2023). FRSs have also continued to be involved in other legal partnerships, including local Crime and Disorder partnerships, Local Safeguarding Boards and Health and Wellbeing Boards. However, obligations and opportunities to collaborate under LSPs significantly reduced following abolition of LSPs and LAAs in 2010 (Murphy & Greenhalgh, 2018).

Understandings of legal accountability when collaborating with the police differed across the two governance models. FRSs that transferred to the PFCC governance model felt accountable to the police under the same governing body, as they have been working together to achieve the same objectives and shared similar governance structures. On the other hand, notwithstanding the legal duty of collaboration, those services that remained under the FRA governance model did not feel legally accountable to the police because of different governance arrangements between the two services. However, they did feel professionally accountable to the police. Similarly, FRSs under both governance models did not perceive the relationship with ambulance services as a legal accountability relationship due to different governance structures between the two services.

Diagonal Accountability

Legal requirements in the form of diagonal accountability have been strengthened as result of the Policing and Crime Act 2017, which revived a FRSs' inspectorate. In this subsection, the legal accountability from the inspectorate is discussed in more detail.

Independent Inspectorate

The Policing and Crime Act 2017 has enhanced external scrutiny arrangements for FRSs through the establishment of HMICFRS. The inspectorate's role is to individually assess effectiveness, efficiency and use of people in all 44 English FRSs. Any services that receive an inadequate rating receive a letter from the inspectorate with recommendations on how to improve, followed by a revisit later in the year. Nevertheless, HMICFRS, like the Audit Commission before, is not able to intervene in the services that have been graded as inadequate, as this power is reserved to the Secretary of State (Home Office, 2018). Generally, the inspectorate's role is to encourage improvement by inspecting and benchmarking all 44 services and identifying and publishing areas of good or notable practice.

FRSs believed that the establishment of inspectorate has increased accountability within and outside FRSs because the inspectorate started to create a national set of expectations that services are expected to meet, which facilitates better benchmarking across services. Interestingly, FRSs started to feel more accountable to central government because of the national inspection process. This was mainly because of the requirement imposed on FRSs to provide data returns and information as part of the inspection process. The inspectorate uses the data not only to report on individual services performance but also to inform their national approach and the government's 'reform' agenda. The inspection process has therefore influenced both government policy and the fire sector's direction of travel. However, some interviewees felt that services did not feel directly accountable to the inspectorate because of its role on services' improvement rather than compliance with regulations.

> *They're an independent body that reports into government, and they are here to report back on our progress. So, they are not our masters...We're not accountable to them but we work with them on our improvement agenda, and they independently report against our progress. (ACFO 2, Case Study 3)*

> *There's data requirements coming out of our ears from HMICFRS, although those are essentially obligations, not sort of legal requirements. (Area Manager 1, Case Study 4)*

> *We have to satisfy them [HMICFRS requirements], but don't want to be slaves to them. (CFO, Case Study 5)*

HMICFRS cannot enforce compliance based upon the results of their inspection reports. However, FRSs are legally obliged to receive any inspection visit from the inspectorate. FRSs felt obligated through the inspectorate to other actors, including the government, other services and the public based on their inspection results. This is because the inspectorate independently reports and recommends the government on all FRSs in the annual report on the 'State of Fire and Rescue'.

Some FRSs, however, questioned the independence of the inspectorate (e.g., Area Manager 1, Case Study 1; Area Manager 1, Case Study 4). This is because HMICFRS claimed to be independent of central government.

However, senior managers did not feel like there was true independence between the two bodies because in practice, the government has been responsible for appointing the HMICFRS inspectors and the Chief Inspector.

> *The government appoint the HMICFRS inspectors and when they sign the report on the state of the fire report, again it is supposed to be independent, but it doesn't feel very independent, some of the things that they do feel politically motivated. (Area Manager 1, Case Study 1)*

HMICFRS has also its budget and financing determined by the Home Office rather than by Parliament or by an independent body (Murphy, 2017; Murphy et al., 2020). This according to participants undermined the inspectorate's independence.

CONCLUSION

This chapter discussed FRSs' understandings of legal accountability before and after the introduction of the Policing and Crime Act 2017. Table 6 summarises FRSs' understandings of legal accountability in relation to vertical, horizontal and diagonal directions.

Legal accountability within FRSs has been primarily associated with the vertical dimension of accountability, enshrined in the statutory requirements, including primary and secondary legislation focused upon FRSs. Over the years, the legislation has changed, but the core statutory requirements for FRSs have remained relatively stable. Legal accountability has also cascaded down to individuals within FRSs responsible for individual statutory roles. The introduction of the PFCC governance model has changed statutory requirements to include additional reporting mechanisms to the central government and amendments to statutory officers' roles in the PFCC-governed services.

FRSs have also been accountable for financial compliance and audits. Before 2010, FRSs were accountable for both their operational and financial audits to the Audit Commission. However, legal accountability significantly changed after the abolition of the Audit Commission and the introduction of austerity-localism. In theory, FRSs remained legally accountable to the government solely for financial conformance. Legal accountability for operational performance shifted towards professional accountability under the sector-led improvement regime (see Chapter 6). Operational performance

Table 6. FRSs' Understandings on Legal Accountability Before and After the Introduction of the Policing and Crime Act 2017.

		Before the 2017 Act	After the 2017 Act	
Directions	**Main Sub-Themes**	**FRA-Governed Services**	**FRA-Governed Services**	**PFCC-Governed Services**
Vertical (central govt/auditing bodies – FRS)	Statutory requirements	*Moderate* accountability through compliance with primary and secondary legislation	*Moderate* accountability through compliance with primary and secondary legislation	*Extensive* accountability through compliance with additional primary and secondary legislation
	Financial compliance	*Moderate* accountability to the government and local communities for standalone FRAs *Limited* accountability to the government and local communities for county council FRA	*Moderate* accountability to the government and local communities for standalone FRAs *Limited* accountability to the government and local communities for county council FRA	*Moderate* accountability to the government and local communities
	Audit	*Extensive* accountability through operational and financial audits until 2015 (Audit Commission) *Limited* accountability through financial audits since 2015 (NAO)	*Limited* accountability through financial audits (NAO)	*Limited* accountability through financial audits (NAO)
Horizontal (FRS – other partners)	Legal partnerships	*Limited* accountability between fire and police and fire and ambulance services	*Limited* accountability between fire and police, and fire and ambulance services	*Moderate* accountability between fire and police *Limited* accountability between fire and ambulance services
Diagonal (inspectorate – FRS)	Inspection, National state of fire reports	*Moderate* accountability under external inspections (1947–2010) *Limited* accountability under the sector-led improvement (2010–2017)	*Extensive* accountability under external inspections since 2017	*Extensive* accountability under external inspections since 2017

Source: Author's interpretation.

was not centrally scrutinised until the 2017 Act and the establishment of HMICFRS, which meant that FRAs became less legally accountable for service outputs and outcomes than was previously the case.

Before the Policing and Crime Act 2017, FRSs felt limited legal horizontal accountability to collaborate with other partners although relatively informal and discretionary collaborative engagements at the local level had been developing since the 1990s. The abolition of LSPs and LAAs, however, weakened horizontal accountability, as it removed partnerships between central government and local areas, in which FRSs were actively involved. This however changed as result of the 2017 Act, which introduced a legal duty on FRSs to collaborate with other emergency services, where such agreements would be in the interests of its efficiency or effectiveness. As a result, FRSs felt more legally accountable to collaborate with the police under the PFCC governance model, primarily because of joint governance arrangements with the police. In contrast, FRA-governed services did not feel legally accountable to collaborate with the police and did not perceive collaboration with ambulance services, as a legal accountability because of the different governance arrangements between the services.

FRSs also felt diagonally accountable via external inspectorates to other stakeholders between 1947 and 2010 and since 2017. Between 2010 and 2017, there was no external inspectorate to oversee their performance. Instead, they were involved in sector-led improvement initiatives, which ultimately resulted in relatively weak accountability towards other stakeholders. With the introduction of the Policing and Crime Act 2017, operational performance accountability has been reinstated diagonally, rather than vertically, through the establishment of HMICFRS.

As result of the Policing and Crime Act 2017, FRSs generally perceived greater legal accountability at various levels under both governance models introduced by the Policing and Crime Act 2017. However, they had mixed views on whether the legal accountability arrangements that this legislation introduced were as strong as the previous Audit Commission regime.

REFERENCES

Coleman, P. (2009). *Fire and rescue improvement: A report prepared for DCLG on the approach and lessons learned 2005–2009*. Fire and Rescue Improvement Support Team, DCLG.

Department for Communities and Local Government (DCLG). (2008). *Fire and rescue service national framework 2008–11*. Communities and Local Government Publications.

Department for Communities and Local Government (DCLG). (2012). *Fire and rescue national framework for England*. DCLG.

Ewen, S. (2009). *Fighting fires: Creating the British fire service, 1800–1978*. Palgrave.

Ferry, L., & Eckersley, P. (2015). Accountability and transparency: A nuanced response to Etzioni. *Public Administration Review*, *75*(1), 11–12.

Home Office. (2018). *Fire and rescue national framework for England*. Home Office.

Lowndes, V., & Pratchett, L. (2012). Local governance under the coalition government: Austerity, localism and the 'Big Society.' *Local Government Studies*, *38*(1), 21–40.

Martin, S. (2000). Implementing 'best value': Local public services in transition. *Public Administration*, *78*(1), 209–227.

Murphy, P. (2017). Independent inspectorate in danger of becoming Home Office handmaiden. *Fire*, *112*(1398), 9–11.

Murphy, P. & Greenhalgh, K. (Eds.). (2018). *Fire and rescue services: Leadership and management perspectives*. Springer.

Murphy, P., & Lakoma, K. (2020, October). Picking apart the PCCs: Two-part review of the role of police, fire and crime commissioners. *Fire*, 15–17.

Murphy, P., & Lakoma, K. (2021). Debate: Public audit, the Redmond Review, and the use of public interest reports. *Public Money & Management*, *41*(2), 150–151.

Murphy, P., & Lakoma, K. (2023). How did fire and rescue services (and HMICFRS) in England respond to the COVID-19 pandemic? *International Journal of Emergency Services*, *12*(1), 77–90.

Murphy, P., Lakoma, K., Eckersley, P., Dom, B. K., & Jones, M. (2023). Public goods, public value and public audit: The Redmond Review and English local government. *Public Money & Management*, *43*(3), 242–250.

Murphy, P., Lakoma, K., Eckersley, P., & Glennon, R. (2020). *Rebuilding the fire and rescue services: Policy, delivery and assurance*. Emerald Publishing.

Office for Public Service Reform (OPSR). (2003). *Inspecting for improvement*. Cabinet Office.

Office of the Deputy Prime Minister (ODPM). (2004a). *The Fire and Rescue Service National Framework 2004/05*. Office of the Deputy Prime Minister.

Office of the Deputy Prime Minister (ODPM). (2004b). *The fire and rescue national framework 2005/06*. Office of the Deputy Prime Minister.

Office of the Deputy Prime Minister (ODPM). (2006). *The fire and rescue national framework 2006–08*. Office of the Deputy Prime Minister.

Public Accounts Committee (PAC). (2016). *Financial sustainability of fire and rescue services: Twenty-third report of Session 2015–2016*. TSO.

Raynsford, N. (2016). *Substance not spin: An insider's view of success and failure in government*. Policy Press.

Romzek, B. S., & Dubnick, M. J. (1987). Accountability in the public sector: Lessons from the Challenger tragedy. *Public Administration Review*, *47*(3), 227–238.

6

FINDINGS: PROFESSIONAL ACCOUNTABILITY

ABSTRACT

This chapter examines the dynamics of professional accountability within English Fire and Rescue Services (FRSs) before and after the governance reforms introduced by the Policing and Crime Act 2017. Using Romzek and Dubnick's (1987) framework, it explores vertical, horizontal and diagonal accountability relationships and their changes under two governance models: Fire and Rescue Authorities (FRAs) and Police, Fire and Crime Commissioners (PFCCs). Prior to 2017, professional accountability was primarily operationalised through training, fitness standards and adherence to public service values, with limited external scrutiny. Horizontal accountability relied on voluntary collaboration and sector-led peer reviews, which proved largely ineffective. Diagonal accountability was minimal due to the absence of a dedicated fire inspectorate and reliance on voluntary guidance. After the introduction of the 2017 legislation, reforms strengthened professional accountability through the mandatory collaboration duty, the establishment of His Majesty's Inspectorate of Constabulary and Fire & Rescue Services (HMICFRS) and the introduction of National Operational Guidance and professional standards. High-profile incidents such as the Grenfell Tower fire and the Manchester Arena bombing further increased expectations for professionalism and fire safety within FRSs. While reforms enhanced standardisation and external oversight, challenges remained regarding collaboration with ambulance services and professional development opportunities.

Keywords: Professional accountability; fire and rescue services; governance reform; public administration; directions of accountability

INTRODUCTION

Following the analysis of legal accountability relationships in Chapter 5, this chapter focuses on the dynamics of professional accountability in English Fire and Rescue Services (FRSs), where perceptions of accountability change as result of governance reforms introduced by the Policing and Crime Act 2017. Professional accountability stresses the power and control in the hands of skilled and expert members of a professional or an expert group who are accountable to agency leaders. Professional bodies and qualifications, such as those that accountants, lawyers and doctors obtain, demonstrate their belonging to the profession. If professionals fail to meet their professional expectations, the professional body can reprimand them or strike them off. In contrast to bureaucratic accountability, where the emphasis is on close supervision (Chapter 3), professional accountability relies on standards, values, technical knowledge and expertise but in an unsupervised context (Mulgan, 2000). Close bureaucratic control from outside the organisation is therefore inappropriate in a professional accountability relationship. Professional accountability relationships are similar to those between a layperson and an expert (Romzek & Dubnick, 1987). Professional accountability is based on a principal–agent relationship with a knowledge asymmetry between the parties (Sharma, 1997). The layperson is an individual who has insufficient knowledge about how the expert should do a job. Nonetheless, professionals still have their ultimate accountability to their superiors (Romzek & Dubnick, 1987).

Professional accountability is more about individual professionals than the service as a whole. In FRSs, firefighters act as skilled and expert employees who fight and prevent fires and protect their communities by utilising their professional knowledge and experience. They have professional pride in carrying out their job, and at the same time, they uphold the ethical standards of the profession. This in turn earns respect from colleagues, the public and other stakeholders, who call them to account based on how the professional standards are operationalised in practice. However, accountability within FRSs does not only apply to firefighters but also to other professionals who work in management and in the 'back office'.

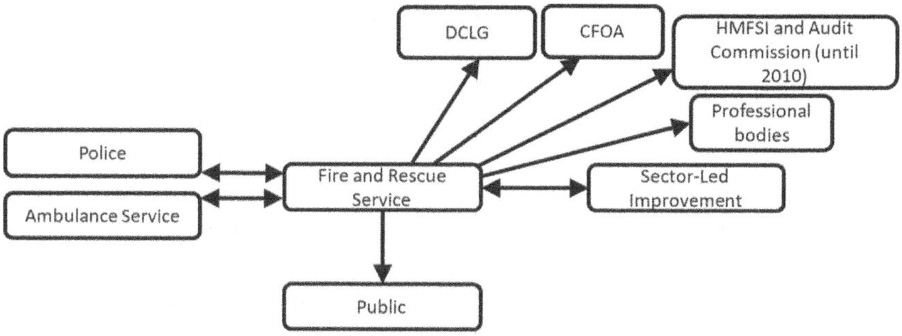

Source: Author's interpretation.

Fig. 9. Fire and Rescue Services' Understandings of Professional Accountability Relationships in FRA-Governed Fire and Rescue Services Before the Introduction of the Policing and Crime Act 2017.

This chapter describes FRSs' understandings of professional accountability in relation to the vertical, horizontal and diagonal directions of accountability, which address the '*accountability for what*' and '*accountability to whom*' dimensions of the conceptual framework, introduced in Chapter 2. More specifically, this chapter examines how these understandings have changed in the context of the governance reforms brought in by the Policing and Crime Act 2017 (see Figs. 9 and 10).

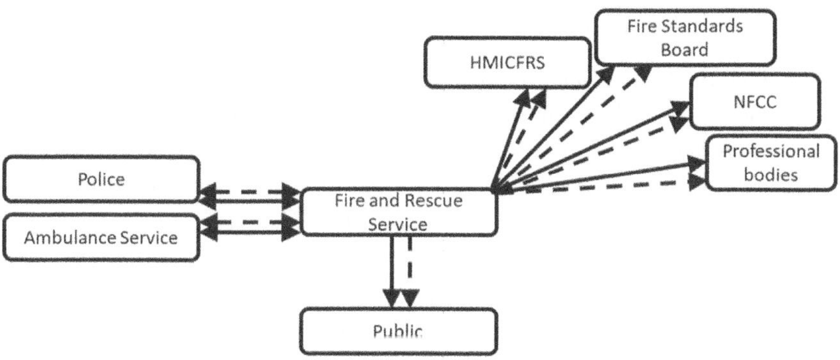

Source: Author's interpretation.

Fig. 10. Fire and Rescue Services' Understandings of Professional Accountability Relationships in FRA-Governed (Solid Lines) and in PFCC-Governed (Dotted Lines) Fire and Rescue Services After the Introduction of the Policing and Crime Act 2017.

ACCOUNTABILITY ARRANGEMENTS PRIOR TO THE POLICING AND CRIME ACT 2017

Vertical Accountability

This subsection explains how professionalism was operationalised in terms of vertical accountability before the introduction of the Policing and Crime Act 2017. In this section, the sub-themes of day-to-day responsibilities and values and principles are discussed within the vertical dimension of professional accountability prior to the introduction of the Policing and Crime Act 2017.

Day-To-Day Responsibilities

FRSs are primarily accountable for carrying out operational duties to local communities. These include fighting fires, protecting and preventing life and property in the event of fire, and rescuing people in case of other emergencies. When responding to incidents, a chain of command operates within the service (Andrews et al., 2014). Firefighters, who are at the bottom of this chain, attend incidents and carry out fire safety work with the public. Above them, crew managers and watch managers attend small incidents whereas station managers, group managers and area managers attend large scale and major incidents. Senior managers indicated that they felt accountable to their front-line colleagues who respond to emergencies for providing them with the right equipment and making sure that they are competent, professional and able to respond in a timely manner.

> *I am the head of paid service, responsible as principal adviser to the FRA [Fire and Rescue Authority] in terms of them discharging their statutory duties. I'm responsible for all the maintenance and management of staff, equipment, operational response, capability, physical human assets. (CFO, Case Study 1)*

> *[We are accountable] to the service users, i.e., those that require the service, we have a duty of care to make sure that our crew is all competent, professional and able to respond with the right equipment and in a timely manner. (Head of Assurance, Case Study 6)*

In turn, firefighters, who are at the front-line of response, felt accountable for following the standards and utilising the knowledge gained at training when responding to emergencies.

I think for me personally, accountability comes through the training that I do and my ability to follow procedures and the standards and the training that we receive...if I'm training to a high standard and I'm keeping up those standards when I'm out at a job or at an incident, then I'm accountable for my actions in that way I guess. (Firefighter, Case Study 3)

Front-line staff indicated that undertaking additional training gave them an advantage of a bigger skillset when responding to emergencies. Technical standards on day-to-day FRSs' operations have been regularly changing because of new innovative approaches and technologies. Training therefore enables firefighters to understand these new technologies and new equipment in their job. Firefighters, as well as higher-level managers, have been educated through various training exercises to make appropriate decisions in extreme emergencies.

Firefighters indicated that they generally relied on their professional knowledge when in emergencies. However, as professionals, they were able to deviate from standard protocols, if necessary, depending upon the nature of the emergency they were responding to.

You know if I make a decision operationally, I've made a decision based on what I can see, information I receive ... what I know in my gut, prior experience. (Firefighter, Case Study 3)

Prior to the introduction of the Policing and Crime Act 2017, there were no professional entry requirements in England to become a firefighter (Wankhade & Murphy, 2023). A firefighter's job is primarily physical and requires high levels of fitness rather than professional qualifications. Newly recruited firefighters begin their job with an intensive training period, which is followed by an ongoing learning and development programme. This culminates in firefighters taking a fitness assessment to ensure that they maintain the standards of physical fitness to perform their role. However, according to the Firefighter Fitness Addendum to the 2012 National Framework for FRSs in England (DCLG, 2014), no individual would be dismissed if they failed the fitness assessment; instead, they would be given a minimum 6 months to regain the necessary levels of physical fitness. If they did not, the FRA was responsible for finding an alternative employment for the individual. Firefighters' professional accountability was therefore operationalised through training, fitness assessments and carrying out their operational duties.

Values and Principles

As public sector organisations, FRSs and their staff are funded by taxpayers. This means that they are required to follow values and principles that are enshrined in the public service. In England, they are known as 'Nolan Principles of Public Life' (Committee on Standards in Public Life, 1995) and include the following: selflessness, integrity, objectivity, accountability, openness, honesty and leadership. Everyone in the public service, including the staff of FRSs, is expected to abide by them.

Firefighters and senior managers felt professionally accountable in terms of their personal exercise of judgement. If a firefighter made a wrong decision at an incident, this would affect their sense of professional responsibility and pride (notwithstanding any additional sanction they may experience through bureaucratic accountability processes). Discussing what went wrong was a form of an evaluation process for the staff. The basis of this would be the individual's personal sense of morality, involving moral values – the Nolan Principles.

Both firefighters and senior managers indicated that they abide by these values. However, only one participant (senior manager) explicitly acknowledged that they follow the Nolan Principles.

> *People should be able to hold me personally to account, both as a role model in the fire service but also a leader delivering an important public service…things like the Nolan Principle, people should read those I think sometimes in terms of their role as in public life. So, I feel accountable all the time. (DCFO, Case Study 1)*

FRSs felt ultimately accountable to communities as they were acting in their interest. They were not only accountable for the operational elements of their job but also for the professional elements. In most case studies, senior managers, as well as front-line staff, adhered to the Nolan Principles in their day-to-day job by exhibiting them in their own behaviour. This included promoting and supporting the principles, as well as challenging inadequate behaviour. Senior managers felt that they could be challenged by local communities for potential abuse of moral values within the service. This occurred in one case study when senior management abused the public's trust, when taking a fraudulent decision in order to gain financial benefits for themselves. This resulted in a number of whistle-blowing complaints about the service and the public's trust, needed to be rebuilt within as well as outside the service.

Horizontal Accountability

Professional accountability can also operate horizontally, in which equal parties use their professional experience to operate or collaborate in mutual areas of interest. This subsection explains how horizontal accountability was operationalised before the 2017 legislation at both organisation and individual levels.

External and Internal Collaboration

Before the introduction of the duty to collaborate in the Policing and Crime Act 2017, local FRSs were involved in a number of external collaborations, most notably with the police and ambulance services, but also occasionally with a wider variety of organisations, and consequently had to act in a professional way when collaborating. For example, FRSs felt professionally accountable to other organisations for training and preparing to respond to emergencies using their knowledge and expertise under the Civil Contingencies Act 2004. Similarly, they were also professionally accountable to police and other local authorities when providing services or undertaking activities within the provisions of the Crime and Disorder 1998 legislation.

FRSs have also been involved in the Joint Emergency Services Interoperability Programme (JESIP), established in 2012, to work with police and ambulance services during major or catastrophic events (Daniels, 2019). In 2014, the programme changed its name to the Joint Emergency Services Interoperability Principles. Its main aim has been to remove over-bureaucratic procedures and work with other emergency services when training and responding to incidents (Wilsher, 2019). FRSs noted that they were mainly involved in the JESIP initiatives at the front-line levels. JESIP formalised multi-agency response to major emergencies and forced individual emergency services to develop plans on how to save lives using their own operational competence, policies and procedures. However, participants also pointed out that all three emergency services work differently.

> *Part of our job is to train, so we train all the time, we're still available for calls etc, but it's part of our role, where the police and the ambulance service for instance, when they're on duty, they're dealing with incidents, they've got workloads that don't allow them to train, so their training comes as an addition. (Firefighter, Case Study 2)*

Participants highlighted that all three emergency services prioritise their workloads and trainings differently, which made it difficult to arrange training sessions together. Nonetheless, horizontal accountability relationships between emergency services at an organisation level continued to develop as FRSs have been designated a core local partner. The increasing complexity of individual incidents and increases in the scale of incidents require emergency services to use their professional experience and collaborate in their response. FRSs felt that engagement in external collaborations was the right thing to do because it improved their skills and knowledge and ultimately helped them to do their jobs better.

Although the theme of accountability through supervision was one of the most recurring in the bureaucratic dimension of accountability (see Chapter 3), a perception of accountability for one's actions was also seen as a distinct theme in terms of professionalism. Professional accountability was evident at the individual level when working together within teams at the front line. Firefighters used their knowledge and expertise gained through trainings to hold each other to account for how they responded to incidents.

> *We're all equally as important and responsible for one another's action, how we train and how we develop ourselves, and it's all in our best interests to help each other, be accountable for each other, how we can improve each other. (Firefighter, Case Study 3)*

Participants also indicated that they felt professionally accountable to their colleagues at the senior management level, as they were working together to achieve the mutual goal of an effective and efficient public service.

> *I also feel I'm accountable to my staff and colleagues so that as the individual, they can and should hold me to account, and say well you said you'd do this, or you were supposed to look after that and it's about making sure that you uphold what you're there to do. And if you are doing that, then they rightly should be saying you've either not delivered or you've let the side down. (Director of Prevention and Protection, Case Study 6)*

Senior managers believed that their colleagues could act as internal peers who can challenge them based on professional knowledge and expertise if their work was insufficiently or inadequately delivered, and consequently, they could learn and improve from their feedback.

Sector-Led Improvement and Organisational Peer Review

Prior to the Policing and Crime Act 2017, FRSs were subject to the Local Government Association's (LGA) peer challenge process, which was part of the sector-led improvement arrangements introduced in 2010 (Downe et al., 2013; LGA, 2011). As part of these arrangements, each service could invite another service to undertake an independent review that would conclude in a report identifying which areas needed improvement. The process was voluntary and consisted of a self-assessment and an external peer challenge by a team of fellow professionals from other fire services and the LGA who reviewed the service using their professional expertise (Downe et al., 2018). Almost all English FRSs were involved in the process although participation was not compulsory. The idea was to have an opportunity to invite peer experts to examine the service with a professional expertise and a different 'pair of eyes' over the problems that services might be experiencing and ultimately exchange information on how they could improve in the future.

In all cases, FRSs reported inadequate accountability under the peer challenge regime. Inspected services would typically get a good report because they could choose which other service would carry out the review and pick the areas that they would examine.

> *It was very rare you didn't get a good report to be honest, because you steered the inspection team down into what you wanted them to see. (ACFO 2, Case Study 4)*

Participants found peer assessments to be biased. The LGA approach was expected to strengthen FRSs' professionalism. In practice, peer assessments did not contribute to the professional improvement of the service nor help staff undertake their jobs better. In addition, the findings of peer challenges were not shared at the national level, and they had limited influence internally within the sector. The assessments were supposed to improve accountability at the local level (Downe et al., 2013, 2018; LGA, 2011). However, the evidence shows that the results of peer challenges were neither robust nor transparent, and after an initial period, when they appeared on the LGA website, they were taken down and were shared only internally. Other FRSs did not hold the reviewed service to account for improvement based on the recommendations. Although the process relied on the professional knowledge and expertise of a peer service, it proved to be an ineffective tool for holding services accountable, even against metrics and targets that they would set themselves.

Diagonal Accountability

While outside professional organisations or inspectorates may diagonally (indirectly) advise the services through inspection reports, education and professional standards, the source of professional accountability remains internal within the service. This subsection explains how diagonal professional accountability was operationalised before the 2017 legislation in FRSs.

Independent Inspectorate

Between 1947 and 2006, FRSs were inspected by His/Her Majesty's Fire Service Inspectorate (HMFSI), and in 2006, the Audit Commission took on the role of external inspection. After the announcement of the abolition of the Audit Commission, England remained without a professional inspectorate for the fire service for next 8 years (Murphy et al., 2020). Professional accountability of FRSs through inspectorates was therefore very limited, particularly after the closure of the Audit Commission.

Operational Guidance

Before the introduction of the Policing and Crime Act 2017, FRSs were not obliged to follow mandatory professional guidance or standards within the fire sector. It was a matter for each service to decide whether they wished to adopt and follow the available guidance, although operational guidance did form part of the sector-led improvement process. For example, the Chief Fire Officers Association (CFOA), which acted as the professional collective voice of the UK FRSs, published various operational guidance, for instance on managing the physical fitness of firefighters, and on fire and risk assessments. The government also published operational guidance, for example, on creating an Integrated Risk Management Plan (IRMP) (DCLG, 2008) to ensure a consistent quality approach across all services. Similarly, other practical reports on operational guidance were published for consideration by FRSs, including operational risk information (DCLG, 2012) and health and safety at work practices (DCLG, 2013). DCLG, as the government's department overseeing FRSs at the time, did not hold responsibility for the application of the guidance but rather indirectly influenced the services' professional approach, as professional standards were a matter for the services themselves. Many services attempted to adopt voluntary guidance, although most of them ended up with mixed results and performing as they saw fit rather than according to the published protocols.

Professional Qualifications and Memberships

Professional qualifications and memberships of other professional bodies have been indirectly influencing the decision-making of FRSs. FRSs' staff have been members of various professional bodies, through which they gain professional expertise and knowledge. Firefighting as a profession does not require individuals to hold specific professional qualifications. Nonetheless, firefighters seek to develop their professional knowledge and expertise of the fire sector by joining professional membership bodies, such as the Institution of Fire Engineers (IFE), or Certified Fire Investigator Programme (CFI), which both shape the fire and rescue sector's professionalism around the world.

The Fire Service College was also responsible for providing various courses for senior fire officers. Until 2013, the College was run by the government's department (DCLG), providing a wide range of courses on leadership, management and operational training. However, in 2013, the college was privatised, and its remit consequently reduced. Similarly, the Emergency Planning College offered various training exercises for large scale civil emergencies, but it was outsourced in 2010, and the UK Government reduced its remit.

FRSs have also been delegating professional accountability to professionally qualified support staff in a diverse range of back-office roles, including finance, procurement, estates, human resources and occupational health. Individuals in these roles attend professional training courses to develop and maintain skills for their specific professions, which offer an accredited level of expertise. Various professional bodies regulate these qualifications and offer international-recognised professional memberships. Senior support staff have been using their professional knowledge and behaviours, gained through professional qualifications and subsequent professional memberships, to demonstrate their commitment to the professional standards within their fields, and to guide and train more junior colleagues.

ACCOUNTABILITY ARRANGEMENTS POST THE POLICING AND CRIME ACT 2017

Vertical Accountability

This section discusses the understandings of vertical bureaucratic accountability under the sub-themes of day-to-day responsibilities, and values and principles, in the FRA governance model (the representation model) and the

Police, Fire and Crime Commissioner (PFCC) governance model (the governance model) following the implementation of the Policing and Crime Act 2017.

Day-To-Day Responsibilities

FRSs have continued to be professionally accountable for their day-to-day duties, including response to incidents, protection and prevention after the introduction of the Policing and Crime Act 2017. According to FRSs, day-to-day service delivery, in both FRA and PFCC governance models remained relatively the same as before the 2017 legislation. FRSs continued to deliver the service according to professional standards, which are set out in their service delivery plans. Firefighters continued to engage in professional development activities, including training courses, to keep up to date with professional advancements in the fire sector. The 2017 legislation has not changed anything with regard to firefighters' training requirements and physical assessments, and firefighters did not notice a change in their day-to-day responsibilities.

However, FRSs have begun to pay increasingly more attention to fire safety after the Grenfell Tower fire in London in 2017 (Moore-Bick, 2019) and the Manchester Arena bombings in 2017 (Kerslake, 2018; Prosser & Taylor, 2020; Saunders, 2021, 2022, 2023). Both incidents, according to participants, at both senior management and front-line level, changed the way FRSs operate, plan and train. This in turn meant that policies and training packages needed to be revised as a result of both incidents. This triggered further high-profile debates about proposed changes to the Fire Safety Order legislation and other high-rise buildings regulations. Local communities also began to take more interest in fire safety matters. The Grenfell Tower fire and the Manchester Arena bombings, which both resulted in high profile and long-running public inquiries (Hackitt, 2017; Kerslake, 2018; Moore-Bick, 2019; Saunders, 2021, 2022, 2023), made local communities and the media across England more aware of how they can hold FRSs to account for poor operational responses to incidents. The public started questioning fire safety, especially fire safety in high-rise residential buildings. This had an impact on FRSs' accountability for ensuring that local areas are adhering to fire safety standards. FRSs consequently strived to achieve high standards as a fire service and therefore aimed at expanding their knowledge on fire safety prevention.

> *Accountability for me is that the public, you're accountable to the public... but also it's the case of now that what's happened with the media, with Grenfell, the public are asking a hell of a lot more questions about things you know and they're interested in more. (Firefighter, Case Study 1)*

> *And I would say there's two good examples, Grenfell and the Manchester Arena...The public expect us to do more...There is lots of criticism for the Greater Manchester FRS and the London [Fire Brigade], because when they needed them in their most life-threatening situations, they did not meet public expectations. (ACFO, Case Study 5)*

These major incidents have influenced FRSs' professionalism. They led the government, the media and the public to expect and demand higher standards of professionalism than had been demonstrated in response to these two incidents.

Values and Principles

FRSs' stance on values and principles remained relatively unchanged compared to their views before the introduction of the Policing and Crime Act 2017. Both front-line as well as senior managers have been required to follow the professional values and principles that are enshrined in public service. FRSs continued to be concerned for the public interest and generally follow the Nolan Principles in terms of professional employee's behaviour. This in turn meant that members of the public have had their right to make complaints if they believed that FRSs or particular individuals do not follow the values and principles of public life.

Horizontal Accountability

FRSs continued to be horizontally accountable and mutually dependent – externally on peer organisations and internally on their colleagues – after the introduction of the Policing and Crime Act 2017. This subsection explains how horizontal professional accountability has been operationalised since the introduction of the 2017 legislation.

External and Internal Collaboration

The Policing and Crime Act 2017 articulates a desire for stronger collaboration across emergency services. The 2017 legislation requires all emergency services to actively investigate further opportunities for joint or collaborative delivery of their services. Nonetheless, most fire services had already been collaborating with other emergency services prior to the 2017 legislation, as result of their legal obligations. In practice, the 2017 legislation has broadened FRSs' collaboration with police services into some new areas. FRSs that remained under the FRA governance model have been acting towards other emergency services, especially the police, as professional peers. This is because they have been mutually dependent on each other when sharing expertise and practices to keep communities safe.

> *It's [the 2017 legislation] made us more aware of being involved around buying, training and other things. When we do management training, in the past perhaps we wouldn't have thought of each other, whereas now we do, and we share initiatives and try and involve each other and have that cross-pollination of ideas. (DCFO, Case Study 3)*

The 2017 legislation has encouraged FRSs to re-explore all possible approaches to collaboration. Front-line staff thought that FRSs had gained a better understanding of the professional needs of other emergency services since they have started to officially collaborate. This is because in the past, FRSs focused entirely on their individual needs when planning for future emergencies. After the introduction of the Policing and Crime Act 2017, this perception changed, as FRSs have been increasingly looking out for greater collaborative approaches with other emergency services and been trying to understand their respective needs.

> *As an arson reduction officer, you've got a skill in the police that can assist fire reduction, you've got skills in the fire that can assist anti-social behaviour reduction. So, there's a lot of benefits from combining. (Area Manager 1, Case Study 3)*

FRSs referred to the benefits that they have been able to provide to other services whilst other emergency services in return have been made more aware of FRSs' needs to operate better. Consequently, emergency services collaboration has become more efficient and effective than previously. Nonetheless, FRSs believed that there is still scope to help other services. For example, by being involved at low-level police incidents. This would free up capacity for the police to go to more important incidents.

FRSs that moved to the PFCC governance model also indicated that they have been mutually dependent on police forces when sharing estates or responding to incidents. FRSs have also become engaged in breaking in through people's homes to save lives, and they have also started supporting missing person's enquiries (Case Study 5). Both the FRA- and the PFCC-governed services, however, indicated that working together with the police services was perceived as an organisational culture change for the staff.

> *The police have got their brand and culture, the fire service have got ours, and I think it's important for both to keep those. We can join up how we work to make those efficiencies and improvements, however from my experience of bringing together a police and fire team on a small scale, it's organisational culture. (Area Manager 2, Case Study 4)*

FRSs are much smaller organisations than police forces. FRSs, both senior managers and front-line staff, feared losing their professional identity when working with the police. This is because the collaboration between the two services mostly relies on FRSs assisting the police, not vice versa. The fear of loss of identity was also expressed by participants when speaking about sharing headquarters with the police. This all contributed to FRSs' reluctance to fully collaborate with police services as they believed that the two services should be equal partners in collaboration.

In both FRA and PFCC governance models, the horizontal accountability relationship between FRSs and ambulance services has been limited. This is because ambulance services are primarily focused on day-to-day response, operate on a regional basis and have little organisational capacity to carry out training exercises. This means that they are unable to invest the resources into proactive collaboration with FRSs. However, there are some examples of greater collaboration between the two services. For example, both services have been engaged in emergency planning through the Local Resilience Forums. They also actively collaborated when FRSs assisted both ambulance services and the NHS to respond to incidents and with the vaccination roll-out during the COVID-19 pandemic (Murphy & Lakoma, 2023). However, both front-line officers and senior managers in FRSs acknowledged that there is scope for greater support from their side to support ambulance services in life saving interventions.

> *We are highly trained up to almost paramedic technician level, all our firefighters are, we carry a lot of first line first aid equipment, and we go to car crashes and significant incidents and give first aid trauma management, we can respond to cardiac arrests, strokes, things like that, and bring people back to life, lots of capacity that we could use to support the ambulance service, who are really struggling with their demands.* (ACFO, Case Study 2)

Senior managers argued that FRSs could support already stretched ambulance services' demand and capacity and ultimately could add more value and help across the emergency services sector. Nonetheless, ambulance services, according to participants, were not convinced that support from FRSs during the pandemic could be sustained in the future. This is because FRSs and ambulance services have different governance arrangements – ambulance services are within the NHS structures – which was seen as a barrier to strengthening collaboration between the two services.

Diagonal Accountability

This subsection explains diagonal professional accountability after the introduction of the Policing and Crime Act 2017. It discusses how the independent inspectorate, professional standards and operational guidance, and professional qualifications and memberships have been operationalised in the fire sector since the 2017 legislation.

Independent Inspectorate

The Policing and Crime Act 2017 established His Majesty's Inspectorate of Constabulary and Fire & Rescue Services (HMICFRS) as a new inspectorate for FRSs after eight years of having no professional fire inspectorate. Senior managers and front-line staff welcomed the creation of the inspectorate, which was intended, inter alia, to influence the quality of services through professional knowledge and expertise, using professional teams, including experienced officers and other fire and rescue experts, to identify best practice in the sector. Senior managers found that the learning and feedback that came from inspection visits and reports did help to improve the quality of services to local communities. Managers indicated that the three pillars of effectiveness, efficiency and people are particularly useful to understand how services can further improve, based on the inspectorate's professional judgement. In particular, the assessment of the 'people' part of inspections includes developing and maintaining a workforce that is professional, resilient, skilled and flexible. The inspection methodology assesses current and future skills requirements and addresses capability gaps within the services. The inspectorate has also been assessing whether the senior leaders of local FRSs are positive role models and whether this is reflected in the collective behaviour of the workforce (HMICFRS, 2024).

The inspection methodology demonstrated that the inspectorate has been professionally influencing FRSs to achieve continuous improvement through learning and development. Participants indicated that the inspectorate brought standardisation of assessment to FRSs, as previously, under the peer review regime, services had greater autonomy under the policy of austerity-localism, and there was hardly any accountability to anybody.

> *The positives of the inspectorate is the standardisation and the ability for the sector to make progress because it brings everybody together and actually localism just meant everyone was going in a different direction, so HMICFRS as an inspectorate allows us all to align and make progress together in one direction. (Area Manager 2, Case Study 3)*

The inspectorate has introduced standardisation of assessment for FRSs, irrespective of the governance model. The annual 'State of Fire' report published by HMICFRS also contributes to professional improvement of FRSs, as it assesses services individually and nationally, and provides an overall view of the sector with specific national recommendations.

Professional Standards and Operational Guidance

The development of a wider range of professional standards and national operational guidance for FRSs has been a key element of the government's fire reform programme since 2017. The National Framework (Home Office, 2018) states that professionalism of FRSs needs to be enhanced through a coherent and comprehensive set of professional standards across all areas of FRSs. Before the establishment of the Fire Standards Board, the National Fire Chiefs Council (NFCC) created new National Operational Guidance, which provided operational good practice in response to incidents. FRSs relied on the operational guidance to ensure that they act appropriately. Both senior managers and front-line staff welcomed the National Operational Guidance initiative as it has started the process of standardisation of operational guidance. The introduction of the operational guidance meant that all FRSs in England have been required to follow the professional protocols, which minimise discrepancies between the way that services operate. FRSs also argued that by implementing the national guidance, they might benefit from closer professional collaboration with other FRSs that have adopted the same procedures as well as generate potential savings from sharing good practice.

When it comes to fire standards, some of them have been developed based on previous guidance, where appropriate. However, several new standards have also been introduced. The Fire Standards Board, with an independent chair, has been set up by the NFCC to develop the standards for the fire sector. Since then, all FRSs have been required to adhere to the standards introduced by the Fire Standards Board and the inspectorate has had regard to these standards as part of their inspections. Senior managers felt that the establishment of the new standards body supported the standardisation agenda of the fire sector.

> *I think with the fire standards coming in, that will be the measure…like the police, there needs to be that national direction and standards for us to be measured against. And we're just going through that messy transition phase to get to that. (Area Manager 2, Case Study 4)*

Senior managers welcomed the establishment of professional standards, not least as an opportunity to share good practice with all fire services, notwithstanding their differences in governance arrangements. At the time of writing (January 2026), the Fire Standards Board had approved 19 professional standards, including some operational standards relating to protection, prevention and risk management. Although the standards have been relatively recently established, FRSs welcomed the change towards coherent and professional priorities for the fire sector.

Professional Qualifications and Memberships

Professional qualifications and memberships continued to indirectly influence the professionalism of FRSs. Professional accountability continued to concern both professionally qualified support staff and operational staff. Both the Fire Service College and the Emergency Planning College remained responsible for providing various training courses although their remit and offering have significantly reduced since privatisation and outsourcing respectively. The scope of professional expertise and knowledge gained through fire education has therefore diminished in the fire sector.

CONCLUSION

This chapter discussed the services' understandings of professional accountability before and after the introduction of the Policing and Crime Act 2017. Table 7 summarises FRSs' understandings of professional accountability in relation to vertical, horizontal and diagonal directions.

FRSs before the 2017 Act were vertically professionally accountable to communities for providing them with the fire safety service. They followed professional standards when responding to incidents, protecting and preventing communities but also adhered to professional values and principles enshrined in the public service. FRSs' professional accountability has not significantly changed as result of the Policing and Crime Act 2017. However, major incidents that occurred in 2017 resulted in FRSs paying increasing attention to fire safety within local areas and ultimately taking a different approach to professional response, planning and training.

FRSs before the 2017 legislation were horizontally accountable and mutually dependent, externally on peer organisations and internally on their colleagues. Externally, firefighters and managers used their professional knowledge and expertise to collaborate with other FRSs and other emergency services to ensure public safety and health and well-being of communities by addressing different incidents and emergencies. They felt that engaging in external collaborations was the right thing to do and ultimately helped them to do their jobs better. Nonetheless, peer challenges were viewed as insufficient in holding services professionally to account. The introduction of the Policing and Crime Act 2017 formalised the duty to collaborate with other emergency services, particularly the police, and encouraged it into wider areas, including closer working relationship in a form of professional accountability. In the cases of the PFCC governance model, this broadened into joint decision-making with the police. Whilst FRSs extended their collaboration with the police in a number of areas, collaboration with ambulance services (except during COVID-19) remained limited due to the different organisational capacities and governance arrangements between two services. Peer challenges were significantly wound down with the establishment of the new inspectorate. Professional accountability also remained

Table 7. FRSs' Understandings of Professional Accountability Before and After the Introduction of the Policing and Crime Act 2017.

		Before the 2017 Act	After the 2017 Act	
Directions	**Main Sub-Themes**	**FRA-Governed Services**	**FRA-Governed Services**	**PFCC-Governed Services**
Vertical (FRS - communities)	Day-to-day responsibilities	*Moderate* accountability for high quality professional response, planning and training	*Extensive* accountability for high quality professional response, planning and training	*Extensive* accountability for high quality professional response, planning and training
	Values and principles	*Extensive* adherence to Nolan principles	*Extensive* adherence to Nolan principles	*Extensive* adherence to Nolan principles
Horizontal (FRS – other fire services/emergency services/partners)	External and internal collaboration	*Moderate* accountability to other emergency services when addressing different incidents and emergencies *Extensive* accountability when working together within teams at the front-line	*Extensive* accountability to the police when addressing different incidents and emergencies *Moderate* accountability to the ambulance services when addressing different incidents and emergencies *Extensive* accountability when working together within teams at the front line	*Extensive* accountability to the police when addressing different incidents and emergencies *Moderate* accountability to the ambulance services when addressing different incidents and emergencies *Extensive* accountability when working together within teams at the front line
	Peer review regime	*Limited* professional accountability through peer challenges	N/A	N/A

Diagonal (Inspectorate/ professional bodies – the service)	Inspectorate	*Limited* accountability towards inspection bodies	*Extensive* accountability towards the inspectorate	*Extensive* accountability towards the inspectorate
	Professional standards/ guidance	*Limited* accountability under operational voluntary guidance (limited fire standards)	*Moderate* accountability under the professional guidance and standards (still emerging)	*Moderate* accountability under the professional guidance and standards (still emerging)
	Professional qualifications and memberships	*Extensive* range of professional training opportunities	*Limited* range of professional training opportunities	*Limited* range of professional training opportunities

Source: Author's interpretation.

important when working together within internal teams at the front-line as firefighters continued to use their knowledge and expertise to hold each other professionally to account.

Before the introduction of the Policing and Crime Act 2017, there was relatively limited diagonal professional accountability within FRSs. Historically, FRSs were diagonally influenced by the professional inspection regime that was abolished in 2010. They were also affected by the operational guidance from the fire sector and professional qualifications and memberships within the service. Generally, they all had limited influence on the professionalism in the fire sector after 2010. The Policing and Crime Act 2017 established a professional inspectorate, inter alia, to assess the professionalism as well as the performance of FRSs. In addition, National Operational Guidance and professional fire standards have been created, which indirectly influence the services' practice and mitigate potential discrepancies between the way that services operate across the sector. The scope of professional education through government agencies has, however, reduced as the two government organisations supporting the fire sector professionalisation were privatised. Nonetheless, FRSs felt greater professional accountability under the new regime introduced by the 2017 legislation, as it has brought benchmarks, standardisation and the potential for the sector to make progress on greater professionalisation within the service.

Overall, the Policing and Crime Act 2017 has brought a number of changes in FRSs' professional accountability. Generally, mechanisms to ensure professional accountability have been extended. The changes affected both FRA- and PFCC-governed services with only marginal differences between them. PFCC-governed services clearly engaged in professional collaboration with police as result of new governance arrangements. On the other hand, collaboration with ambulance services remained limited for both types of governance models, due to the different organisational capacities between the two services.

REFERENCES

Andrews, R., Ashworth, R., & Meier, K. J. (2014). Representative bureaucracy and fire service performance. *International Public Management Journal*, *17*(1), 1–24.

Committee on Standards in Public Life. (1995). *Standards in public life: First report of the Committee on Standards in Public Life*. HMSO.

Daniels, C. (2019). Emergency services architecture: JESIP and interoperability. In P. Wankhade, L. McCann, & P. Murphy (Eds.), *Critical perspectives on the management and organization of emergency services* (pp. 15–29). Routledge.

Department for Communities and Local Government (DCLG). (2008). *Integrated risk management planning: Guidance*. https://www.gov.uk/government/collections/integrated-risk-management-planning-guidance

Department for Communities and Local Government (DCLG). (2013). *Fire and Rescue Authorities: Health, safety and welfare framework for the operational environment*. TSO.

Department for Communities and Local Government (DCLG). (2014). *Addendum to the fire and rescue national framework for England: Firefighter fitness*. DCLG.

Downe, J., Martin, S., & Doering, H. (2013). *Supporting councils to succeed: Independent evaluation of the LGA's corporate peer challenge programme*. Local Government Association.

Downe, J., Martin, S., & Doering, H. (2018). Peer challenge: A sector-led approach to performance improvement in Fire and Rescue Services. In P. Murphy & K. Greenhalgh (Eds.), *Fire and rescue services: Leadership and management perspectives* (pp. 61–75). Springer.

Hackitt, J. (2017). *Building a safer future: Independent review of building regulations and fire safety – Interim report*. TSO.

His Majesty's Inspectorate of Constabulary and Fire and Rescue Services (HMICFRS). (2024). *How we inspect fire and rescue services*. https://hmicfrs.justiceinspectorates.gov.uk/fire-and-rescue-services/how-we-inspect-fire-and-rescue-services/

Home Office. (2018). *Fire and rescue national framework for England*. TSO.

Kerslake, R. (2018). *The Kerslake Report: An independent review into the preparedness for, and emergency response to, the Manchester Arena attack on 22 May 2017*. TSO.

Local Government Association (LGA). (2011). *Taking the lead: Self-regulation and improvement in local government*. LGA.

Moore-Bick, M. (2019). *Grenfell Tower Inquiry: Phase 1 report – Report of the Public Inquiry into the fire at Grenfell Tower on 14 June 2017 (HC 49-1)*. TSO.

Mulgan, R. (2000). 'Accountability': An ever-expanding concept? *Public Administration*, *78*(3), 555–573.

Murphy, P., & Lakoma, K. (2023). How did fire and rescue services (and HMICFRS) in England respond to the COVID-19 pandemic? *International Journal of Emergency Services*, *12*(1), 77–90.

Murphy, P., Lakoma, K., Eckersley, P., & Glennon, R. (2020). *Rebuilding the fire and rescue services: Policy, delivery and assurance*. Emerald Publishing.

Prosser, T., & Taylor, M. (2020). *The Grenfell Tower fire: Benign neglect and the road to avoidable tragedy*. Pavilion Publishing and Media.

Romzek, B. S., & Dubnick, M. J. (1987). Accountability in the public sector: Lessons from the Challenger tragedy. *Public Administration Review*, *47*(3), 227–238.

Saunders, J. (2021). *Manchester Arena Inquiry: Volume 1: Security for the Arena*. https://www.gov.uk/government/publications/manchester-arena-inquiry-volume-1-security-for-the-arena

Saunders, J. (2022). *Manchester Arena Inquiry: Volume 2: Emergency response*. https://www.gov.uk/government/publications/manchester-arena-inquiry-volume-2-emergency-response

Saunders, J. (2023). *Manchester Arena Inquiry: Volume 3: Radicalisation and preventability*. https://www.gov.uk/government/publications/manchester-arena-inquiry-volume-3-radicalisation-and-preventability

Sharma, A. (1997). Professional as agent: Knowledge asymmetry in agency exchange. *Academy of Management Review*, 22(3), 758–798.

Wankhade, P., & Murphy, P. (2023). *Emergency services management: A research overview*. Routledge.

Wilsher, R. (2019). Personal reflections on Fire and Rescue incident command. In P. Wankhade, L. McCann, & P. Murphy (Eds.), *Critical perspectives on the management and organization of emergency services* (pp. 52–69). Routledge.

7

CONCLUSION: SHIFTING ACCOUNTABILITY IN FIRE AND RESCUE SERVICES – THEORY AND PRACTICE

ABSTRACT

This chapter summarises how governance reforms introduced by the Policing and Crime Act 2017 reshaped accountability in English Fire and Rescue Services (FRSs). It compares accountability dynamics under the traditional Fire and Rescue Authority (FRA) model and the Police, Fire and Crime Commissioner (PFCC) model, using Romzek and Dubnick's typology (1987) and Bovens' accountability directions (2007). Findings reveal that reforms aimed to strengthen political accountability through directly elected PFCCs, alongside enhanced bureaucratic, legal and professional accountability via new accountability mechanisms such as inspections and statutory collaboration duties. This chapter highlights the complex interplay between accountability types and directions, offers policy and practice recommendations and argues that accountability remains a contested concept requiring balanced mechanisms and further research to address persistent governance challenges. This chapter also discusses the UK Government's emerging preference for the directly elected mayoral governance model as part of ongoing efforts to achieve more direct local accountability.

Keywords: Accountability; fire and rescue services; governance reform; public administration; public governance

INTRODUCTION

The aim of this book has been to understand how notions of accountability change depending on the way public services are governed. In particular, this study compared Fire and Rescue Services' (FRSs') understandings of accountability before and after the governance changes brought about by the Policing and Crime Act 2017, by focusing on the differences between accountability in the new Police, Fire and Crime Commissioner (PFCC) governance model services, in the traditional Fire and Rescue Authority (FRA) governance model services and in the latter after it was refined by the 2017 Act.

All FRSs generally shared similar understandings of accountability before the introduction of the Policing and Crime Act 2017, as they were all governed by their local FRAs. However, although FRSs from combined and metropolitan FRA models had very similar understandings of accountability, FRSs that were governed by county council FRAs had slightly different perspectives on accountability (see Chapter 5). This is because combined and metropolitan FRAs acted as standalone governing bodies whereas those services that were governed by county council FRAs were embedded in the county council's leadership and management structures. Standalone FRAs were therefore directly legally accountable for financial compliance to the government and local communities whereas county council FRAs were indirectly legally accountable to government and local communities, because their primary relationship was with the county council.

Following the introduction of the Policing and Crime Act 2017, FRSs experienced a number of governance changes. Most notably, some services moved to the PFCC governance model. As a result, FRSs' understandings of accountability have changed as result of the new governance arrangements. Moreover, these changes resulted in different understandings of accountability in FRA-governed services, on the one hand, and PFCC-governed services, on the other hand (see Figs. 11 and 12 for comparison).

In relation to the vertical direction of accountability, FRSs that remained under the FRA governance model after 2017 felt moderate bureaucratic accountability from their FRA. In contrast, FRSs that transferred to the PFCC governance model experienced extensive bureaucratic accountability from their new governing bodies – the PFCCs. Similarly, FRSs believed that the FRA governance model offered moderate level of political accountability when it comes to dismissing the members of FRAs whereas PFCC governance model provided extensive political accountability as result of the directly elected individual overseeing the service. However, the PFCC governance

Accountability for what?

Accountability to whom?

Direction	Bureaucratic accountability	Political accountability	Legal accountability	Professional accountability
Vertical	**Limited** scrutiny from an FRA. **Moderate** accountability from top to bottom through meeting performance targets.	**Limited** ability to dismiss FRA members. **Limited** opportunities for the public to engage with the services. **Moderate** transparency. **Moderate** level of connections with local areas and communities.	**Moderate** accountability through compliance with legislation. **Extensive** accountability through operational and financial audits until 2015. **Limited** accountability through financial audits since 2015.	**Moderate** accountability for high quality professional response, planning and training.
Horizontal	**Limited** accountability relationship when collaborating with police and ambulance services.	**Moderate** level of mutual accountability working towards policies and strategies.	**Limited** accountability between fire and police, and fire and ambulance services	**Moderate** accountability to other emergency services. **Limited** professional accountability through peer challenges.
Diagonal	**Limited** accountability towards inspection bodies or peer organisations.	**Moderate** level of influence of political parties and representative bodies on FRAs' decision-making.	**Moderate** accountability under external inspections (1947-2010), **Limited** accountability under sector-led improvement (1947-2010)	**Limited** accountability towards the inspectorate. **Limited** accountability under operational voluntary guidance. **Extensive** range of professional training opportunities.

Governance reforms since 2017

Accountability for what?

Accountability to whom?

Direction	Bureaucratic accountability	Political accountability	Legal accountability	Professional accountability
Vertical	**Extensive** scrutiny from the PFCC. **Extensive** accountability through performance-oriented structures within services.	**Extensive** ability to dismiss the PFCC. **Extensive** opportunities for the public to engage with the services. **Limited** transparency. **Limited** level of connections with local areas and communities.	**Extensive** accountability through compliance with legislation. **Limited** accountability through financial audits.	**Extensive** accountability for high quality professional response, planning and training.
Horizontal	**Moderate** accountability relationship when collaborating with police. **Limited** accountability relationship when collaborating with ambulance services.	**Extensive** level of mutual accountability working towards policies and strategies.	**Moderate** accountability between fire and police **Limited** accountability between fire and ambulance services.	**Extensive** accountability to the police. **Moderate** accountability to ambulance services.
Diagonal	**Extensive** bureaucratic scrutiny of the inspectorate focused on performance.	**Extensive** level of influence of political parties and representative bodies on PFCCs' decision-making.	**Extensive** accountability under external inspections.	**Extensive** accountability towards the inspectorate. **Moderate** accountability under operational voluntary guidance. **Limited** range of professional training opportunities.

Source: Author's own interpretation of the level of accountability in this study.

Fig. 11. FRA-Governed Services: Summary of Fire and Rescue Services' Understandings of Accountability Before and After the Introduction of the Policing and Crime Act 2017.

Accountability for what?

Accountability to whom?

Direction	Bureaucratic accountability	Political accountability	Legal accountability	Professional accountability
Vertical	**Limited** scrutiny from an FRA. **Moderate** accountability from top to bottom through meeting performance targets.	**Limited** ability to dismiss FRA members. **Limited** opportunities for the public to engage with the services. **Moderate** transparency. **Moderate** level of connections with local areas and communities.	**Moderate** accountability through compliance with legislation. **Extensive** accountability through operational and financial audits until 2015. **Limited** accountability through financial audits since 2015.	**Moderate** accountability for high quality professional response, planning and training.
Horizontal	**Limited** accountability relationship when collaborating with police and ambulance services.	**Moderate** level of mutual accountability working towards policies and strategies.	**Limited** accountability between fire and police, and fire and ambulance services.	**Moderate** accountability to other emergency services. **Limited** professional accountability through peer challenges.
Diagonal	**Limited** accountability towards inspection bodies or peer organisations.	**Moderate** level of influence of political parties and representative bodies on FRAs' decision-making.	**Moderate** accountability under external inspections (1947-2010). **Limited** accountability under sector-led improvement (1947-2010).	**Limited** accountability towards the inspectorate. **Limited** accountability under operational voluntary guidance. **Extensive** range of professional training opportunities.

Governance reforms since 2017

Accountability for what?

Accountability to whom?

Direction	Bureaucratic accountability	Political accountability	Legal accountability	Professional accountability
Vertical	**Moderate** scrutiny from an FRA. **Moderate** accountability from top to bottom through meeting performance targets.	**Moderate** ability to dismiss FRA members, including the PCC. **Limited** opportunities for the public to engage with the services. **Moderate** transparency. **Moderate** level of connections with local areas and communities.	**Moderate** accountability through compliance with legislation. **Limited** accountability through financial audits.	**Extensive** accountability for high quality professional response, planning and training.
Horizontal	**Limited** accountability relationship when collaborating with police and ambulance services.	**Moderate** level of mutual accountability working towards policies and strategies.	**Limited** accountability between fire and police, and fire and ambulance services.	**Extensive** accountability to the police. **Moderate** accountability to ambulance services.
Diagonal	**Extensive** bureaucratic scrutiny of the inspectorate focused on performance.	**Moderate** level of influence of political parties and representative bodies on FRAs' decision-making.	**Extensive** accountability under external inspections.	**Extensive** accountability towards the inspectorate. **Moderate** accountability under operational voluntary guidance. **Limited** range of professional training opportunities.

Source: Author's own interpretation of the level of accountability in this study.

Fig. 12. PFCC-Governed Services: Summary of Fire and Rescue Services' Understandings of Accountability Before and After the Introduction of the Policing and Crime Act 2017.

model offered limited political accountability with regard to the transparency of decision-making and the level of connections with local communities whereas the FRA governance model provided moderate political accountability with regard to these factors. When it came to legal accountability, FRSs that transferred to the PFCC model experienced extensive legal accountabilities of statutory compliance with additional legislation whereas FRA-governed services felt that their legal accountabilities remained relatively similar to those before the Act and were therefore moderate. In terms of professional accountability, both FRA- and PFCC-governed services felt extensive accountability to local communities for how they respond, plan and train.

Horizontally, FRSs that remained under FRAs continued to feel limited bureaucratic and legal accountability when collaborating with police and ambulance services despite the statutory duty to collaborate with other emergency services. In comparison, those services that transferred to the PFCC governance model experienced moderate bureaucratic and legal accountability to the police and limited bureaucratic and legal accountability when working with ambulance services. PFCC-governed services felt that joint governance arrangements with the police contributed to greater accountability between the two services. All FRSs believed that the different governance arrangements at the horizontal level hindered their accountability to their partners. Similarly, when it came to political accountability, PFCC-governed services felt extensive accountability between politicians and officers holding each other to account whereas FRA-governed services felt moderate accountability to the local councillors in FRAs. In terms of professional accountability, FRA-governed services felt moderate accountability when collaborating with the police and ambulance services whereas those services that transferred to the PFCC governance model experienced extensive professional accountability when working with the police and moderate professional accountability to ambulance services, partially as result of joint governance with the police.

Diagonally, both FRA- and PFCC-governed services experienced extensive bureaucratic, legal and professional accountability, primarily through the establishment of the inspectorate. This is a change from the situation before the 2017 reforms, when diagonal accountability was relatively limited in bureaucratic, legal and professional areas. In terms of political accountability, FRSs felt an indirect moderate influence from political parties and representative bodies in FRA-governed services but more extensive influence in PFCC-governed services.

The findings show that FRSs' understandings of accountability differed before and after governance reforms in relation to '*accountability for what*' and '*accountability to whom*'. Perhaps unsurprisingly, those services that transferred to the PFCC governance model experienced greater changes in understandings of accountability as result of the 2017 legislation than those services that remained under the FRA governance model. However, both FRA- and PFCC-governed services generally felt more accountable to their stakeholders in comparison to the situation before the Policing and Crime Act 2017.

This chapter provides an in-depth analysis of how and why FRSs' understandings of accountability have shifted following the introduction of the Policing and Crime Act 2017. More generally, it examines how and why governance reforms reshape accountability dynamics within public services, drawing on the literature reviewed in Chapter 2 and the empirical findings presented in Chapters 3–6.

INTERPRETATION OF EMPIRICAL FINDINGS

In recent decades, governments have introduced various reforms to try to improve public accountability (Dubnick & Yang, 2011). Although the complex and qualitative nature of both governance arrangements and accountability mean it is difficult to measure the extent to which they have achieved this, studies have nonetheless shown that governance reforms can lead to changes in the various forms of accountability.

One issue associated with investigating accountability under governance reforms is therefore not only understanding whether they enhance accountability or not but also understanding how accountability is perceived by different actors (Romzek, 2000). This book has argued that accountability is often perceived in terms of two dimensions – '*accountability for what*' (bureaucratic accountability, political accountability, legal accountability and professional accountability) and '*accountability to whom*' (vertical accountability, horizontal accountability and diagonal accountability). It has used both dimensions to demonstrate that public services manage combinations of multiple, different, changing and often conflicting and overlapping expectations within and outside their organisations (Acar et al., 2008; Willems & Van Dooren, 2011).

Romzek (2000) argues that in times of reform there are usually calls for a reliance on a 'different kind' of accountability. For example, Romzek and

Dubnick (1987) found that the space shuttle Challenger tragedy in 1986 happened because of over-reliance on political and hierarchical (bureaucratic) accountabilities rather than adequate or sufficient professional accountability. Similarly, Kim (2005), in a study of non-profit community mental health centres, found that excessive legal and hierarchical (bureaucratic) accountability may have a detrimental effect on professional and political accountabilities. These examples demonstrate that satisfying multiple accountability demands can prove to be highly challenging.

Both the UK Government and FRSs claimed that FRSs (and the FRAs) required significant reforms as result of poor governance and ineffective accountability structures. As a result, the UK Government responded to perceived accountability problems by introducing new provisions enshrined in the Policing and Crime Act 2017, which simultaneously affected all four types of accountabilities. The example of the Policing and Crime Act 2017 reforms shows that the government decided that the priority for English FRSs was greater political accountability through newly established PFCCs, greater professional and bureaucratic accountability via His/Her Majesty's Inspectorate of Constabulary and Fire & Rescue Services (HMICFRS) and greater bureaucratic and legal accountability through collaboration with other emergency services. The 2017 reforms did introduce a number of new accountability mechanisms although their practical implementation has been perceived by FRSs to be different from the original vision proposed by the government.

First, the 2017 legislation intended to enhance *political accountability* and the community responsiveness of FRSs by establishing directly elected PFCCs. The previous FRA governance model largely corresponded to the bureaucratic type of accountability, operating in a 'committee' style when scrutinising FRSs. The UK Government was concerned over FRAs' insufficient control of FRSs. However, it also claimed that FRSs' greater accountability needed to be exercised at a local level through governing bodies by giving them greater autonomy. English FRSs had no directly elected element in their traditional FRA governance model. The 2017 reforms aimed to re-establish a direct relationship between FRSs and the local communities they serve by introducing a directly elected individual specifically responsible for local FRSs. It was clear that the government originally envisaged that PFCCs would eventually be the predominant form of governance across the sector. Since English FRSs previously had no directly elected element, PFCCs were therefore portrayed as almost a panacea for the previous inadequate governance structures.

In practice, this did not happen, and the new arrangements have largely failed to provide communities with adequate communication channels. This book has found that new reporting arrangements under the PFCC governance model have been less transparent than under the FRA governance model, and PFCCs were generally less responsive to their local communities than FRAs. Additionally, the public's interest in FRSs and the PFCCs' elections have been limited. This was reflected in relatively low voter turnout, e.g., in the 2021 PFCC elections with Essex 50.6%, Northamptonshire 24.9%, Staffordshire 28.2%, North Yorkshire 24.9% (Danechi & Tunnicliffe, 2021) and in the 2024 PFCC elections with Essex 24.9% (Colchester City Council, 2024), Northamptonshire 19.62% (West Northamptonshire Council, 2024), Staffordshire 19.23% (Staffordshire Commissioner, 2024) and Cumbria 21.17% (Cumberland Council, 2024). North Yorkshire had no election (in May 2024, the governance functions of the PFCC transferred to the Mayor of York and North Yorkshire). This shows that the direct political accountability did not necessarily help to reconnect FRSs with their local communities and the level of public's engagement in FRSs has remained relatively low.

The controversies around transferring the democratic mandate from FRAs to PFCCs also contributed to the negative perceptions of FRSs regarding the implementation of the PFCC governance model. However, the Conservative government has been a strong advocate of the PFCC governance model and provided financial support to nine Police and Crime Commissioners (PCCs) to help them develop their business cases (Eckersley & Lakoma, 2022; Home Office, 2017). Nevertheless, by January 2026, after nearly 10 years of government support and encouragement, only five FRSs (Essex, Northamptonshire, Staffordshire, North Yorkshire and Cumbria) had transferred to the PFCC governance model. In three of these areas, Essex,[1] Northamptonshire[2] and Cumbria,[3] extraneous or abnormal factors were a significant influence on the success of the business cases for transfer.

Other potential cases faced significant local opposition, and as a result, the vast majority of FRSs remained under the FRA governance model. This suggests that the implementation of the PFCC governance model has not been carried out as originally intended by the Conservative government. In 2024, there was an election of a new Labour government that remains committed to extending the remit of directly elected individuals overseeing FRSs, and this now includes the transfer of local FRSs' governance to directly elected mayors as part of the government's wider vision of transferring responsibilities to single-person governance models.

In practice, the 2017 reforms did not significantly change the political accountability of FRSs; however, the introduction of PFCCs have had implications for other types of accountabilities. For example, bureaucratic accountability strengthened in both FRA- and PFCC-governed models as the introduction of PCCs/PFCCs brought improved scrutiny of the services. In addition, the governing bodies, responsible for providing political accountability to local communities, could also rely more on the bureaucratic mechanism of inspection reports to scrutinise the services. Political measures of accountability have also affected legal accountability, as the introduction of the PFCC model of governance imposed additional legal responsibilities for services that transferred to the PFCC governance model. Finally, in the services that had transferred to the PFCC governance model, professionalism has increased as they started to collaborate more with police services. The collaboration improved their skills and professional knowledge, and they ultimately become more effective in their roles.

Second, both the government and FRSs acknowledged that too much unjustified reliance was placed on horizontal professional accountability under the sector-led improvement regime before 2017. This is because, inter alia, these horizontal forms of accountability offered limited or zero sanctioning options (Schillemans, 2008, 2011). Sanctions under the sector-led improvement regime were practically non-existent as the peer review regime offered a lack of formal scrutiny and hardly any accountability (Downe et al., 2018; Murphy & Ferry, 2018). FRSs did not robustly hold each other to account for improvement based on the peer review recommendations. Not only was there a need for more robust and extensive accountability arrangements but also a better balance between professional, bureaucratic, political, and legal accountabilities in FRSs. Prior to 2017, the sector argued for a re-introduction of a number of measures of *bureaucratic accountability*, including the establishment of an external inspectorate focused on supporting improvement. As a result of the 2017 legislation, HMICFRS has been providing diagonal accountability, albeit with no direct consequences for FRSs. Nonetheless, the creation of HMICFRS has also had implications for FRSs' professional accountability, as it indirectly influenced the professionalism of FRSs. FRSs started to feel greater professional accountability when the HMICFRS was established because the performance assessments included new professional benchmarks and the potential for the sector to make progress on greater professionalisation within the service. The establishment of a performance management regime through HMICFRS has also influenced the area of legal accountability as it has legally imposed external inspections on services. The increased bureaucratic accountability measures also had an impact on political accountability as it enabled the governing bodies (either FRAs or PFCCs) to hold the service to account for performance based on HMICFRS inspection reports. However, the accountability arrangements, that the 2017 legislation introduced, were not as powerful as the pre-2010 Audit Commission regime that previously held FRSs to account. The inadequacies of FRSs' accountabilities were further illustrated by the Grenfell Tower and Manchester Arena Bombing inquiries, where both professional and bureaucratic accountabilities were insufficient to hold FRSs to account (Hackitt, 2017; Kerslake, 2018; Moore-Bick, 2019; Saunders, 2021, 2022, 2023) and suggested a need for a greater scope of mechanisms to hold FRSs to account.

Third, the government also introduced a legal duty on emergency services to collaborate, if it is in the interests of public safety or their efficiency or effectiveness. This specific provision of the Policing and Crime Act 2017 was primarily intended to enhance two types of accountability – *legal accountability and bureaucratic accountability*. First, it introduced potential consequences for services not following the statutory duty. In practice, FRSs felt limited legal accountability to collaborate with other emergency services partners because they shared this duty (and accountability) with them. Theoretically, the introduction of the statutory duty to collaborate has also had implications for political accountability as it enhanced FRAs and PFCCs scrutiny on compliance with the duty of collaboration. However, FRSs did not feel that the compliance with the duty to collaborate was adequately scrutinised by any of the other actors holding FRSs to account, including FRAs or PFCCs. Furthermore, it was intended to make FRSs bureaucratically accountable for efficiency and effectiveness when collaborating with other emergency services in pursuance of greater public safety. This did happen for PFCC-governed services and their accountability relationships with the police, in that the new model enabled joint decision-making and discussions about potential efficiencies resulting from the collaboration. In addition, it enabled emergency services to be mutually professionally accountable to each other when sharing professional expertise and practices to keep communities safe. However, this was largely limited to relationships with the police under the PFCC governance model. Collaboration between FRA-governed services and the police and all FRSs and the ambulance service remained relatively limited. Different governance arrangements between FRSs and ambulance services remained a significant barrier to horizontal bureaucratic accountability relationship between the two services.

The changes introduced from a professional perspective (the establishment of HMICFRS, the National Fire Chiefs Council (NFCC), and the Fire Standards Board) started to address the previous limited accountability mechanisms prior to the 2017 legislation, including sector-led improvement initiatives, limited professional qualifications and other recognitions within

FRSs. Fire and Rescue personnel ultimately felt the need for more external reassurance that they were doing a good, professional job. The establishment of new professional organisations has indirectly influenced the decision-making of FRSs through education and professional standards. However, as with diagonal accountability, professional accountability remained largely internal within the services, as the new organisations were able to offer their professional expertise but were not able to enforce compliance. Hence the extent of professional accountability of FRSs, in both FRA-governed and PFCC-governed services remains very similar, with scope for development and improvement in both.

The 2017 legislation and government reforms were intended to introduce more extensive accountability mechanisms in FRSs. The 2017 Act has affected all four types of accountabilities to a different extent. This study shows that the Act and the government has focused on some types of accountability more than others. In addition, the empirical findings reveal that a different pattern of accountability types and accountability directions emerged than the government intended, and to varying degrees. In practice, the establishment of the inspectorate has had an extensive legal, bureaucratic and professional influence across all FRSs whereas political accountability of newly established PFCCs has clearly not been as influential or as widespread as anticipated. Seven years after their introduction, only a small number of FRSs have transferred to the PFCC governance model and been subject to direct elections within their areas. On the other hand, all FRSs reported extensive accountability changes as result of the indirect influence of HMICFRS in bureaucratic, professional and legal accountabilities. The establishment of the inspectorate brought back a stronger focus on performance management into the fire sector although initially without taking sufficient notice of the need for professionalisation of the sector. The government's aim was to improve the sector's performance by making FRSs more accountable to an external inspection regime (Power, 1997). However, this has proved more difficult than expected, as the inspectorate's initial approach relied heavily on the current policing inspection model. The inspection framework has, however, been continuously developing as the inspectorate better understands the way in which fire sector operates and is governed. Nevertheless, inadequacies in fire and rescue professionalism remained and the sector (and government) supported a renewed focus on professional accountability, by establishing a professional standards body and transforming the Chief Fire Officers Association (CFOA) into the NFCC.

The empirical findings reveal that the governance reforms and changes in the organisational landscape changed the balance of different types and directions of accountability within FRSs. This book found that a change in one type of accountability has had implications for each of the other types of accountability in FRSs. It demonstrates the complicated and overlapping nature of different accountabilities in FRSs.

The findings also show that the government's vision of accountability in the fire sector differed from the FRSs' understandings of accountability. The 2017 reforms did introduce a number of new accountability mechanisms; however, their practical implementation has been perceived by FRSs to be different from the original vision proposed by the UK Government. This suggests that understandings of accountability depend not only on governance arrangements but also on perceptions of the involved parties. The prospect of further reforms confirms that the new government is still dissatisfied with the post-2017 situation. This may be because ministers cannot agree with the fire and rescue stakeholders on what elements of accountability are important, and therefore how to get the balance between them right, suggesting that accountability in English FRSs remains a contested concept.

THEORETICAL PERSPECTIVES: ACCOUNTABILITY DYNAMICS

Based on a synthesis of Romzek and Dubnick's (1987) and Bovens' (2007) accountability typologies, this book contributes to the public administration literature by suggesting a new approach to analysing accountability understandings in public services as result of governance reforms. It argues that accountability is often perceived in terms of two dimensions – '*accountability for what*' (bureaucratic accountability, political accountability, legal accountability and professional accountability) and '*accountability to whom*' (vertical accountability, horizontal accountability and diagonal accountability) – and uses both to explain the impact of governance reforms on understandings of accountability (see Chapter 2).

Previous studies have primarily focused on explaining Romzek and Dubnick's accountability types (1987) in relation to the traditional vertical direction of accountability. This study has, for the first time, identified accountability mechanisms in relation to all three accountability directions and Romzek and Dubnick's accountability typology (see Table 8). Specifically, it has shown how reforms to the UK public sector, including to FRSs in England, have affected traditional vertical accountability relationships and also created new horizontal and diagonal directions of accountability (Schillemans, 2008, 2011).

Table 8. Summary of Accountability Mechanisms in Relation to Accountability Types and Directions.

	Bureaucratic	Political	Legal	Professional
Vertical	Overview and scrutiny, performance	Elections, decision-making, responsiveness to communities	Legislation, government intervention	Expertise, values, and principles
Horizontal	Effective and efficient collaboration	Working relationships	Legal partnerships	Peer review, professional collaboration
Diagonal	Performance, inspections	Political parties and representation bodies	Legal inspections	Expert scrutiny, professional advice

Source: Author.

Vertical bureaucratic accountability relies on overview and scrutiny, as well as performance metrics. Vertical political mechanisms of accountability include direct or indirect elections and organisation's decision-making and responsiveness to communities. Vertical legal accountability revolves around compliance with primary and secondary legislation, with the threat of government or legal intervention in cases of non-compliance. Vertical professional accountability relies on organisations' expertise, values and principles when being held to account. This suggests that vertical mechanisms of accountability show a clear hierarchical definition of authority between the organisation and the stakeholders holding the organisation to account.

This book has also found that accountability mechanisms are activated in the horizontal direction between parties operating or collaborating in the same areas of interest (Michels & Meijer, 2008). In bureaucratic accountability, parties can hold each other to account for effective and efficient collaboration. In political accountability, parties are accountable to each other when working together to deliver policies and strategies for the organisation. In legal accountability, parties are legally obliged to work in contractually based partnerships. In professional accountability, parties are involved in professional and peer collaboration. These mechanisms, although stressing different types of accountability, show that actors involved in horizontal accountability relationships get the opportunity to become actively involved at a similar level of decision-making although they tend to do it without a clear hierarchical definition of authority.

This study has also found a number of diagonal accountability mechanisms in relation to the accountability types. Diagonal accountability relationships operate in the shadow of hierarchy (Bovens, 2007), with a two-step relation to a forum, in which a third party is independent from the agent and the principal (Schillemans, 2008). In bureaucratic accountability, inspection bodies report to the government and the public on the activities and performance of public services. In political accountability, political parties and representative bodies are the third parties that indirectly influence the organisation's decision-making. As with bureaucratic accountability, legal accountability operates when inspection bodies undertake a mandatory legal inspection on an organisation. In professional accountability, professional bodies and inspectorates report on the organisation's professional conduct.

In practice, horizontal and diagonal accountability mechanisms act as extensions of traditional vertical accountability and operate '*in the shadow of hierarchy*' (Schillemans, 2008). They do not substitute vertical accountability mechanisms but instead serve as an addition to traditional forms of accountability (Michels & Meijer, 2008; Schillemans, 2008, 2011). Previous research has primarily focused on explaining accountability types in relation to the traditional vertical directions of accountability. This study expands the focus of enquiry by analysing all three directions of accountability to generate a more complete understanding of complex governance arrangements and their potential impact on accountability in public sector settings.

The conceptual framework that this study is based on is universal and can be adapted by other public services experiencing governance reforms. It can assist practitioners in understanding inadequacies of accountability in their organisations and generate recommendations on how to improve specific types of accountability. At the same time, it helps highlight that the different types can at times overlap and/or complement each other and suggests that government, public services and sectors should seek to identify the most appropriate balance of accountabilities in their circumstances.

A WAY FORWARD: SINGLE-PERSON GOVERNANCE MODELS

More decentralised leadership arrangements, including the directly elected single-person model of governance, have recently been gaining traction in English local government after a long period of traditional local authority 'committee' or 'board' style representational governance. Many countries outside of the United Kingdom have already established directly elected individuals, especially directly accountable mayors (Eckersley & Timm-Arnold, 2014). The single-person governance models, including directly elected mayors, PCCs and recently PFCCs, have been implemented in the United Kingdom to try to enhance decision-making and improve political accountability to citizens (Fenwick et al., 2006; Lister & Rowe, 2015). These governance changes were specifically intended to enhance local accountability, as they enabled the public to directly hold the elected individuals to account through elections and referendums (Lowndes & Gardner, 2016; Lowndes & Pratchett, 2012). Similarly, the extension of the PCC governance model into the PFCC governance model was also intended to improve the relationship between the services, the politicians and more importantly, the public. However, earlier studies found that more local referendums and public consultations have rejected the single-person governance model than have favoured it (Rallings et al., 2014; Sandford, 2022). In addition, recent studies indicate that the public have often no clear understanding of the directly elected individuals' roles and responsibilities (Ferry & Sandford, 2022; Murphy et al., 2017).

The results of this study largely support the findings of previous studies as they demonstrate that the PFCC governance arrangements, brought in by the Policing and Crime Act 2017 and promoted by central government, were largely opposed by local communities and other key FRSs' stakeholders. Ultimately, in those places where they were implemented, the arrangements did enable communities to have a direct say on who is responsible for the governance of their local FRSs; however, they have provided only limited responsiveness to communities. In contrast, the FRA governance model, based on representative democracy in a traditional 'committee' style, continues to provide greater opportunities for the communities to speak with their local councillors. Nevertheless, despite limited responsiveness to communities, PFCCs have been able to streamline the accountability process by providing a single point of contact for FRSs and potentially improve scrutiny of their local services.

This study demonstrates that although PCCs have been powerful individuals (Eckersley & Lakoma, 2022), their influence has been largely limited in the fire sector because only a small number of FRSs have transferred to the PFCC governance. It argues that the PFCC model has some of the weakest accountability arrangements in subnational governance in the United Kingdom due to its party-political allegiance and inadequate responsiveness to local communities.

Following the 2024 UK general election, the new Labour government confirmed a change that moved ministerial responsibility for all fire policy and functions from the Home Office to the Ministry of Housing, Communities and Local Government (MHCLG). In November 2025, the government announced that the PCCs and PFCCS roles will be scrapped at the end of the electoral cycle in May 2028. The government's view is that the PFCC governance model has not delivered robust enough local accountability and is not widely understood by the public, which reflects the findings of this study. Instead, the government envisages clearer governance arrangements with direct accountability to a single directly elected individual, ideally a 'strategic mayor', who would hold the operationally independent Chief Fire Officer (CFO) to account.

The proposed reforms build on changes set out in the English Devolution and Community Empowerment Bill (July 2025), which establishes mayoral responsibility for policing and FRAs by default where geographical boundaries align. The Bill also allows for a single mayor to assume responsibility for PCC and FRA functions across two or more areas where boundaries coincide. Devolution is also likely to result in the merger of FRSs. Under the proposed framework, elected strategic mayors would be supported by appointed Deputy Mayors in areas where strategic mayoral arrangements are in place. These strategic mayors would be elected universally across the whole of England. In cases, where mayoral elections are delayed, or where combined authority structures do not yet exist, interim arrangements would include Police and Fire Boards made up of local government leaders. FRAs are also expected to continue operating in areas where local authority and combined authority boundaries do not align although the strong implication is that boundaries would subsequently be coterminous.

Consequently, although PCCs and PFCCs are due to be abolished, a single national governance model is unlikely to emerge in the short to medium term. Instead, England is likely to experience a mixed landscape of mayoral oversight, boards and FRAs. While this approach may enhance strategic coordination and visibility in mayoral areas, it also prolongs concerns regarding direct accountability to the public. Further detail on the implementation of these reforms is expected in 2026.

The developments clearly point towards an increasing focus on single-person governance models. The findings of this book provide new theoretical insights to the literature on single directly elected individuals, including the US literature on sheriff governance, which has been long established and often politicised (Baldi & LaFrance, 2013; Sampson, 2012). They extend the understanding of single-person enforcement arrangements at a local level as the US sheriffs do not have a specific police, fire or crime mandate, and their responsibility is generally to hold public sector agencies to account (Mawby & Smith, 2013). However, to fully understand the single-elected governance model, further research, including research from the public's perspective, is needed to examine the impact of directly elected governance and the varieties of its arrangements on accountability.

RECOMMENDATIONS FOR POLICY AND PRACTICE

The safety and security of local communities, the public, Fire and Rescue staff and the staff of their key delivery partners have and will be affected by changes in governance and accountability as result of changing government policies. The findings of this study suggest several courses of action for the UK Government, the representative bodies and FRSs, if they wish to improve governance and accountability arrangements for the fire sector at national, organisational and individual levels.

Recommendations for the Government and Representative Bodies

This book identified a number of inadequacies arising from the provisions enshrined in the Policing and Crime Act 2017 and suggests several recommendations for the UK Government and representative bodies to improve governance and accountability arrangements for FRSs.

First, English FRSs currently operate under various governance models. The findings suggest that having multiple governance models creates complex and varying accountability arrangements for FRSs. A solution to current discrepancies among different models would be the introduction of common governance arrangements across all services. Local FRSs would therefore have the same governance, funding and accountability arrangements, which would enable greater collaboration, benchmarking and sharing good practice between the services. The Labour government's preference is clearly towards directly elected individuals overseeing fire services in the foreseeable future, primarily combined authority mayors (although this would not align them with the governance models in Scotland, Wales and Northern Ireland). This research recommends a single model of governance rather than multiple variations of models. It suggests that a single-person, more apolitical model with extensive transparency and effective scrutiny arrangements could provide more effective accountability to the public and other stakeholders. This is because this study found that a single point of accountability has been more effective in scrutinising services rather than a 'committee' style board of individuals. However, the findings of this study also demonstrate that the proposed single point of accountability (i.e., an individual) ought to be a person that is not affiliated with any political party and be above party-political influence to ensure apolitical decision-making within the service. In effect, such individuals would have to comply with and be added to Schedule 1 of the Local Government Officers (Political restrictions) Regulations 1990. The recommended governance model would also have to provide extensive transparency measures and responsiveness to communities' obligations, both of which would enable local communities to scrutinise their local services.

Second, it is more effective to introduce mutual and several legal duties to collaborate when parties have similar governance arrangements, responsibilities, structures and scrutiny arrangements and cover the same geographic area. This study has shown that collaboration between services that are governed at different levels (e.g., national, regional, or local) remains a significant barrier to improving collaboration. This was the case of collaboration between FRSs and ambulance services, which remained limited following the introduction of the legal duty to collaborate due to the different organisational capacities and governance arrangements between the two services. This study found that FRSs did not feel horizontally accountable to ambulance services. It suggests that having the same governing body (e.g., a PFCC) enables services to collaborate more together and become more accountable to each other. Policymakers and practitioners who wish to facilitate greater collaboration between emergency services should consider introducing reforms such as common governance arrangements, as a way to help achieve this objective.

Third, governing bodies responsible for public service's strategy should ideally be operating in line with the organisational and the public interests. This study revealed that politicians sitting on governing bodies sometimes take decisions that are politically motivated and potentially not in the best interest of services and communities. All participants agreed that emergency services' decision-making should be as apolitical as possible, properly scrutinised and should be focused on maintaining or improving public safety and providing the best service to the public, with minimal political influences. This study found that politicians often felt indebted to their party leaders for their positions and aligned themselves with party-political positions. This enables them to indirectly introduce and implement more of their party-political agenda into local public service delivery. One solution would be to have independent, non-partisan politicians that are not affiliated with any political party, overseeing local public services (independents). In this scenario, the individuals would be selected based on their skills and sector-specific knowledge to oversee a public service rather than political party affiliation.

Finally, there is a greater scope to improve FRSs' accountability through the national bodies involved in representing FRSs, including the HMICFRS, the NFCC, the Fire Standards Board, the Fire Sector Federation and the Fire Brigades Union. FRSs welcomed the introduction of professional standards, more robust data and benchmarking, which, according to the participants, started to improve professional and bureaucratic accountability in the fire sector. However, there is still greater scope to improve their accountability arrangements. This includes the sector's commitment to strengthening professional standards and data within FRSs but also greater clarity regarding a separation between the role of the CFO and the governing body (FRA/PFCC). More specifically, this study suggests introducing the operational independence of CFOs (as currently supported by the HMICFRS and FRSs), with CFOs responsible for making operational decisions and ultimately being held to account for performance of their FRS by their governing bodies, acting as the strategic oversight body.

This book demonstrates that continued efforts are needed to improve current governance and accountability arrangements in FRSs in England and in public services more generally. In particular, political accountability of local governing bodies needs to be strengthened to provide extensive transparency measures and more responsiveness to communities' obligations. Professional and bureaucratic accountability also requires further improvements in terms of more robust data in the fire sector and benchmarking with other services. Nevertheless, this study demonstrates that accountability in English FRSs remains a contested concept that potentially leads to future reforms because the government cannot agree with the fire and rescue stakeholders on what elements of accountability are important and therefore how to get the balance between them right.

Taken together, the recommendations above, if implemented, could have a positive impact on performance of FRSs and ultimately improve the safety and security of local communities, Fire and Rescue staff and the staff of their key delivery partners. These are recommendations that apply to English FRSs; however, they also extend to other public sector organisations with similar governance arrangements (such as the police, local authorities or health and social care system) where improved operational performance and more robust financial arrangements have regularly been called for (e.g., Murphy et al., 2023; Wankhade & Murphy, 2024). They will also have resonance and relevance for FRSs in the devolved administrations.

Recommendations for FRSs

This book also suggests how FRSs can improve their accountability arrangements within their organisations. Table 9 makes some practical recommendations for local FRSs on how they could focus on each of the accountability types to improve accountability within their organisations.

Table 9. Practical Recommendations for FRSs.

	Characteristics	Practical Recommendations for FRSs
Bureaucratic accountability	Scrutiny on performance of delegated duties	• Implement accountability mechanisms focused on robust performance management regimes throughout the organisation • Establish effective communication channels between senior management and front-line staff • Systematically review and improve service performance based on HMICFRS inspection outcomes and external audits, with independent quality assurance of the improvements
Political accountability	Representing local communities and being responsive to their needs	• Engage local communities in planning service design and delivery • Establish a robust accountability relationship with clear operational/strategy division between senior management and FRA/PFCC
Legal accountability	Following statutory legislation	• Assign legal accountabilities at an individual level within an organisation and include as appropriate on the organisational risk register, with periodical reviews by the monitoring officer and potential escalation to the governing body

Table 9. ***(Continued)***

	Characteristics	Practical Recommendations for FRSs
Professional accountability	Using expertise and knowledge to deliver services to local communities	• Collaborate with other emergency services to improve co-ordination, skills and professional knowledge within and across the organisations • Improve professional knowledge based on HMICFRS inspection outcomes and organisational development initiatives • Regularly and formally assess technical skills and professional knowledge within the organisation and undertake gap analysis

Source: Author.

They include recommendations that can be implemented at both the organisational level as well as the individual level.

Overall, this book provides practitioners, including policymakers, the government, representative bodies as well as local FRSs and the individuals working within the fire sector, with recommendations on how to build and maintain an organisational culture of accountability whilst meeting the statutory obligation to continuously improve. It recommends several courses of actions at the national level and at the organisational level to improve accountability arrangements whilst maintaining the most appropriate accountability balances specific to FRSs. Although these recommendations are tailored to English FRSs, they also extend to other organisations operating in the public sector with similar governance arrangements.

FUTURE RESEARCH

As a result of the study, further research could be conducted to paint a more complete picture of the impact of governance reforms on understandings of accountability in public services. This study recommends examining accountability as result of governance reforms from other stakeholders' perspectives. This includes local communities directly affected by governance changes, as well as local politicians involved in governance arrangements (if they experienced the situation before and after the reforms). This would provide a more comprehensive and richer overview and determine whether the public services' understandings differ from those of other stakeholders involved in the governance arrangements.

Further research might also explore accountability understandings as result of governance reforms in other public services, including other emergency services (police and ambulance services) as well as local authorities. More studies from different perspectives would help to establish if other public services experiencing governance reforms perceive accountability in a way similar to English FRSs.

The issue of the directly elected individual governance models and their impact on accountability should also be moved forward nationally and internationally to better understand the implications on accountability relationships in public services. This would enable us to examine the varieties of directly elected individual governance arrangements and determine whether and how understandings of accountability under single-elected politicians vary internationally.

CONCLUSION

This chapter set out to discuss the findings of this study. It summarised and interpreted the empirical findings, which was followed by an analysis and discussion of the theoretical and practical implications of the findings. It then provided recommendations for the fire sector and other public services and future research agenda.

Prior to this study, accountability in FRSs had received relatively little academic attention. Despite the Act's explicit intention to improve accountability in FRSs, no previous studies had examined it empirically from this perspective. Theoretically, the findings of this study contribute to the public administration scholarship by understanding the implications of governance reforms on perceptions of accountability in the public sector. The book has shown that changing the nature of governance arrangements in public services has significant implications for accountability. By contrasting the situations in PFCC-led and FRA-led FRSs, this study has highlighted how different governance arrangements influence the relationships that organisations and individuals are involved in. It has also shown that governance reforms often result in changes to a complicated and overlapping set of different accountabilities in public services. Although it is difficult to measure the concept of accountability (because quantitative measures do not reflect the complexity of governance arrangements within public services), it nonetheless has shown that governance reforms can lead to changes in different nature and dimensions of accountability.

Based on a synthesis of Romzek and Dubnick's (1987) and Bovens' (2007) accountability typologies, this book has proposed a new approach to analysing accountability understandings in public services as result of governance reforms. Although the existing literature has primarily focused on explaining accountability types in relation to the traditional vertical directions of accountability, this study has for the first time identified different accountability mechanisms in relation to Romzek and Dubnick's accountability typology (1987) and has extended it to investigate the three accountability directions (Bovens, 2007). It has argued that accountability is often perceived in terms of two dimensions – '*accountability for what*' (bureaucratic accountability, political accountability, legal accountability and professional accountability) and '*accountability to whom*' (vertical accountability, horizontal accountability and diagonal accountability) – and has used both to explain the impact of governance reforms on understandings of accountability. The framework helps to identify how both dimensions may change as it elucidates accountability understandings before and after the governance reforms.

The 2017 legislation clearly demonstrated that the government reforms aimed to introduce more extensive political accountability mechanisms in FRSs. The empirical findings, however, reveal that the accountability types and accountability directions envisioned by the government have only been realised to limited and varying degrees. In practice, they resulted in a different 'blend' of all different types of accountabilities within the sector.

This study has also shown that there is no ideal trade-off between all types of accountabilities, as perceived by governance actors, because they have different understandings of the concepts involved. Accountability therefore remains a contested concept that often leads to re-interpretation and further reforms. However, in order to reduce the discrepancies between the government's plans for public services and those of the delivery organisations, all stakeholders' perceptions ought to be taken into account by the government when it comes to new legislation for public services.

NOTES

1. In 2015, Essex FRS had been subjected to an independent review which found the service to be a failing organisation with a toxic organisational culture (Lucas, 2015).
2. In 2018, an independent report labelled Northamptonshire County Council as a 'failing organisation' with 'significant financial challenges' (Caller, 2018).
3. Cumbria County Council together with its district councils were re-organised in 2023 (The Cumbria (Structural Changes) Order 2022) with the Ministry of Housing, Communities & Local Government establishing a PFCC, albeit against a popular opinion and vote.

REFERENCES

Acar, M., Guo, C., & Yang, K. (2008). Accountability when hierarchical authority is absent: Views from public–private partnership practitioners. *The American Review of Public Administration*, *38*(1), 3–23.

Baldi, G., & LaFrance, C. (2013). Lessons from the United States sheriff on the electoral selection of police commissioners in England and Wales. *Policing: A Journal of Policy Practice*, 7(2), 148–157.

Bovens, M. (2007). Analysing and assessing accountability: A conceptual framework. *European Law Journal*, *13*(4), 447–468.

Caller, M. (2018). *Northamptonshire County Council best value inspection.* https://www.gov.uk/government/publications/northamptonshire-county-council-best-value-inspection

Colchester City Council. (2024). *Police, Fire and Crime Commissioner election results.* https://www.colchester.gov.uk/elections/pfcc-election-results/

Cumberland Council. (2024). *Police, Fire and Crime Commissioner elections.* https://www.cumberland.gov.uk/voting-and-elections/police-fire-and-crime-commissioner-elections

Danechi, S., & Tunnicliffe, R. (2021). *PCC elections 2021*. House of Commons Library.

Downe, J., Martin, S., & Doering, H. (2018). Peer challenge: A sector-led approach to performance improvement in FRSs. In P. Murphy &

K. Greenhalgh (Eds.), *FRSs: Leadership and management perspectives* (pp. 61–75). Springer.

Dubnick, M. J., & Yang, K. (2011). The pursuit of accountability: Promises, problems, and prospects. In D. C. Menzel & H. E. White (Eds.), *The state of public administration: Issues, challenges and opportunities* (pp. 171–186). Routledge.

Eckersley, P., & Lakoma, K. (2022). Straddling multiple streams: Focusing events, policy entrepreneurs and problem brokers in the governance of English FRSs. *Policy Studies*, *43*(5), 1001–1020.

Eckersley, P., & Timm-Arnold, P. (2014). Directly-elected mayors and the austerity agenda: Lessons from the German experience. *Public Money & Management*, *34*(5), 347–354.

Fenwick, J., Elcock, H., & McMillan, J. (2006). Leadership and management in UK local government: A role for elected mayors? *International Review of Administrative Sciences*, *72*(3), 431–447.

Ferry, L., & Sandford, M. (2022). Developing "place leadership" when hierarchical accountability is omnipresent: The case of English sub-national government. *Journal of Public Budgeting, Accounting and Financial Management*, *34*(4), 557–565.

Hackitt, J. (2017). *Building a safer future: Independent review of building regulations and fire safety (interim report)*. TSO.

Home Office. (2017). *Home Office funds PCCs to support further police and fire collaboration*. https://www.gov.uk/government/news/home-office-funds-pccs-to-support-further-police-and-fire-collaboration

Kerslake, R. (2018). *The Kerslake report: An independent review into the preparedness for, and emergency response to, the Manchester Arena attack on 22 May 2017*. TSO.

Kim, S. E. (2005). Balancing competing accountability requirements: Challenges in performance improvement of the nonprofit human services agency. *Public Performance and Management Review*, *29*(2), 145–163.

Lister, S., & Rowe, M. (2015). Electing police and crime commissioners in England and Wales: Prospecting for the democratisation of policing. *Policing and Society*, *25*(4), 358–377.

Lowndes, V., & Gardner, A. (2016). Local governance under the conservatives: Super-austerity, devolution and the "smarter state". *Local Government Studies*, *42*(3), 357–375.

Lowndes, V., & Pratchett, L. (2012). Local governance under the coalition government: Austerity, localism and the "Big Society". *Local Government Studies*, *38*(1), 21–40.

Lucas, I. (2015). *Independent cultural review of Essex County FRS*. Essex County Fire and Rescue Authority.

Mawby, R. I., & Smith, K. (2013). Accounting for the police: The new police and crime commissioners in England and Wales. *Police Journal*, *86* (2), 143–157.

Michels, A., & Meijer, A. (2008). Safeguarding public accountability in horizontal government. *Public Management Review*, *10*(2), 165–173.

Moore-Bick, M. (2019). *Grenfell Tower Inquiry: Phase 1 report—Report of the Public Inquiry into the fire at Grenfell Tower on 14 June 2017 (HC 49-1)*. TSO.

Murphy, P., Eckersley, P., & Ferry, L. (2017). Accountability and transparency: Police forces in England and Wales. *Public Policy and Administration*, *32*(3), 197–213.

Murphy, P., & Ferry, L. (2018). Another turn of the screw: Fire and rescue under the Coalition Government of 2010–2015. In P. Murphy & K. Greenhalgh (Eds.), *FRSs: Leadership and management perspectives* (pp. 45–59). Springer.

Murphy, P., Lakoma, K., Eckersley, P., Dom, B. K., & Jones, M. (2023). Public goods, public value and public audit: The Redmond Review and English local government. *Public Money & Management*, *43*(3), 242–250.

Power, M. (1997). *The audit society: Rituals of verification*. Oxford University Press.

Rallings, C., Thrasher, M., & Cowling, D. (2014). Mayoral referendums and elections revisited. *British Politics*, *9*(1), 2–28.

Romzek, B. (2000). Dynamics of public accountability in the era of reform. *International Review of Administrative Sciences*, *66*(1), 21–44.

Romzek, B. S., & Dubnick, M. J. (1987). Accountability in the public sector: Lessons from the Challenger tragedy. *Public Administration Review*, *47*(3), 227–238.

Sampson, F. (2012). Hail to the chief? How far does the introduction of elected police commissioners herald a US-style politicization of policing for the UK? *Policing: Journal of Policy Practice*, 6(1), 4–15.

Sandford, M. (2022). *Directly elected mayors (Research briefing)*. House of Commons Library.

Saunders, J. (2021). *Manchester Arena Inquiry: Volume 1: Security for the arena*. https://www.gov.uk/government/publications/manchester-arena-inquiry-volume-1-security-for-the-arena

Saunders, J. (2022). *Manchester Arena Inquiry: Volume 2: Emergency response*. https://www.gov.uk/government/publications/manchester-arena-inquiry-volume-2-emergency-response

Saunders, J. (2023). *Manchester Arena Inquiry: Volume 3: Radicalisation and preventability*. https://www.gov.uk/government/publications/manchester-arena-inquiry-volume-3-radicalisation-and-preventability

Schillemans, T. (2008). Accountability in the shadow of hierarchy: The horizontal accountability of agencies. *Public Organization Review*, *8*, 175–194.

Schillemans, T. (2011). Does horizontal accountability work? Evaluating potential remedies for the accountability deficit of agencies. *Administration & Society*, *43*(4), 387–416.

Staffordshire Commissioner. (2024). *Ben Adams re-elected as Staffordshire Commissioner*. https://staffordshire-pfcc.gov.uk/ben-adams-re-elected-as-staffordshire-commissioner/

Wankhade, P., & Murphy, P. (2024). Resilience and wellbeing: The persistent challenges for our emergency services. *Public Money & Management*, *44*(2), 95–97.

West Northamptonshire Council. (2024). *Election results*. https://www.westnorthants.gov.uk/electoral-services/election-results

Willems, T., & Van Dooren, W. (2011). Lost in diffusion? How collaborative arrangements lead to an accountability paradox. *International Review of Administrative Sciences*, *77*(3), 505–530.

Printed and bound by CPI Group (UK) Ltd, Croydon, CR0 4YY

28/09/2026

14971126-0001